dare to be

DEVOTED

30 Day Devotional

Natalie Grant & Charlotte Gambill

ISBN-10: 0615742645

ISBN-13: 978-0-615-74264-9

dare to be

DEVOTED

30 Day Devotional by Natalie Grant and Charlotte Gambill

This devotional is dedicated to all of the women alongside of us who are Daring to Be...

We would like to give thanks to our fabulous editor Caroline Lusk, our administrators Kristi Brazell and Shirley James, and our designers Mike and Allison Harvie. Without the support of our husbands and children, this dream would not be possible. We love them for cheering us on and for partnering alongside us as we dare to be.

—Charlotte and Natalie

I'd also like to personally thank Caroline Lusk for her help in bringing my thoughts and ideas alive on paper. Without her dedication to this project, it would not have come to fruition.

—Natalie

CONTENTS

dare to be

"Without faith it is impossible to please God."

Hebrews 11 v 6 (NIV)

I will never forget years ago standing in a worship service in California, being so clearly instructed by the voice of God to open my eyes, because the girl at the back of the church I was visiting had to do with my future. I remember at the time looking at this girl, who had no idea I was even aware of her presence and thinking this was one of the strangest things God had ever said to me. Who was this girl and how was she attached to my future? I was left with more questions than answers.

That God whisper became the first of many on a journey of "daring to be." I nervously dared to go and find the girl God had pointed out. I introduced myself and as we began to share our individual journeys with one another, God quickly began to join us on a new journey together. That stranger was Natalie Grant, who has, over time become my best friend. You see before we could dare you to be, we had to first be willing to dare to be.

Daring to step out into the unknown is never easy no matter how young or old you are. We all battle with the same nagging doubts. Is this really you Lord? Is this really your voice or is it just my imagination? We question the timing, the place and even the person God has chosen to use. We doubt our ability to respond and are more aware of the reasons why God shouldn't use us than the reasons why He could. Yet beyond the insecurity and excuses is a realm of new possibilities. If we dare to move past the response of our flesh and let our spirit speak, we will find we are more courageous than we may have realized and we were created for more than we may dare to believe. God has an incredible world for us to embrace and it all begins when we "dare to be."

When God joined our lives, we started by daring to get to know each other and to grow together as wives, moms and friends. Over time, we have discovered that God always has so much more for us than we see for ourselves. It was not long into our friendship that God dared us to take our gifts and use them to reach more people. He dared us to take His message in word and song to women from all backgrounds, to dare them to reach for all God has for their lives. So with an ocean between us, as I live in England and Natalie in the USA, we dared to make plans that would overcome the natural obstacles in our way and bring "dare to be" to life. So with a tour bus loaded up, schedules rearranged, much prayer and a lot of risk, we dared to respond. The journey has only just begun, but it has already taught us so much about the beauty and the craziness that happens when you dare to be! Some of the lessons we have learned, we now want to share with you.

On this journey we have laughed, cried, grown and fallen more in love and awe with our incredible Savior, over and over again. God does some of His best work in some of the scariest places. On the edge of your fear you will find faith. Beyond your comfort you will discover courage and when you give up control you will find the place of sweet surrender.

Daring has taken us from strangers to friends. It has also given us a dream that crossed the oceans and began a new adventure with God. We pray the thoughts we share with you here will become fuel to your faith and strength to your soul. We pray that you would dare to see what God sees and to believe for the more He has for your life. He wants to take you further. His willingness to use you is not in question. His ability to provide for you is limitless. His belief in you is unwavering. All it takes is your willing heart. Go on. Open it to His today. We dare you.

We love you and are praying for you,

Charl and Nat

dare to be FREE

by ng

DARE TO BE *FREE*

"Truly I say to you, everyone who practices sin is a slave to sin. Now a slave has no permanent place in the family; the son remains forever. So if the Son sets you free, you will be free indeed."

John 8:34-36 ESV

Have you ever had a bad habit? Biting your nails, saying hi to Ben & Jerry at 3AM, downing 12 Diet Cokes a day? And come New Years, you resolve that this is the year—no more (fill in the blank with habit of choice). For the first few days, you're on track. The excitement of taking on your latest foe keeps you energized and focused. The next week, though, your adrenaline is beginning to wane a bit and the lure of that cold Diet Coke staring at you through the drink machine at work is getting stronger. Before long, the hold you think you've broken re-emerges and there you go—drinking the soft drink, downing the ice cream, chomping the nails or other such vices. (And yes, I am talking from personal experience!)

Now, when you think about this scenario with rather innocuous images like ice cream or soft drinks, it doesn't seem all that extreme. But what about when those habits are more serious? Even life-threatening? Be it alcohol, drugs, exercise, eating disorders, inappropriate relationships or other, we are extremely vulnerable to addiction. Why? Because we're a people in need. God created us that way. He knew that we were fragile. He knew we needed comfort and strength and refuge. And He provided it...He provides it still.

However, for many of us, we don't like our comfort to be intangible. We'd prefer to lay down a few dollars or send out a text and immediately receive the effects of our drug of choice. Before we even realize it, we have become enslaved to the benefits of instant relief and gratification. We are slaves to our own desires. And while we may not be in chains or behind bars, we are most definitely not free.

While we're in the midst of it, chances are we know that something's off. We know that our minds shouldn't be consumed with what awaits us after dark for our little shot of euphoria. We know that many of our decisions are those we hope our children never witness, much less our God view from on high. Despite those reservations, it's still much too easy to convince ourselves that we're not really hurting anyone else. *We're good people most of the time...this is just our little way of unwinding and disconnecting.*

How easily we believe our own manipulation! This is NOT the life God intended for you or me or anyone. His intent is that we walk freely in the joy of our salvation through Him. He desires to be our refuge. He offers the relief and comfort we need and He daily knocks on our hearts with His hands extended. So why don't we answer? Why don't we embrace His offering? I think it's because we don't really grasp what true freedom looks like. I read once that after the emancipation of slavery, many slaves stayed on the property, working for the same owner for whom they had been. It was familiar. It was convenient and it didn't require the risk of the unknown.

How often do you and I do that very same thing? God has freed us from every snare of this world. By the death of Christ on the cross and the resurrection that followed, we were offered the key that unlocks every chain and tears down every stronghold keeping us from the abundant life we were meant to live. But when we're faced with boldly leaving the slave quarters we've known for so long, for an unmarked, foreign wilderness, it just seems like too much risk. It seems to ask from us more than we can give.

Here's the good news—it's never too late. Even if you have been enslaved to a habit or sin every day of your life, God's offer of freedom is as good today as any other. In our inconsistent attempts to be who we were created to be, God lovingly and consistently offers Himself. I dare you to take what He has and run with it. I dare you to allow what may seem like an intangible offering to break through the chains of earthly voices that still hold you captive.

You and I are FREE. We are NO LONGER slaves to anything. We are HIS. We are LOVED. And HE is more than enough for every hurt that we try to numb or void we try to fill. Trust Him today with your need. And believe that the freedom He offers is always the better option. The only option. You are free. Don't stay in your slave quarters anymore. Live. Love. And claim your freedom today.

YOUR DAILY DARE

1. What in your life is enslaving you?

2. What actions today can you take to begin to break down those strongholds?

3. What are you afraid you will lose by letting go of your habits? Write them down, share them with God and then observe on paper how, overtime, God fulfills those needs.

dare to be

SURRENDERED

by CG

DARE TO BE *SURRENDERED*

"Mary came in with a jar of expensive aromatic oils, anointed and massaged Jesus' feet and then wiped them with her hair."
John 12 MSG

I love to watch athletes race, but I have always thought it funny the starting position each runner has to assume before they can begin the race. It seems strange that their starting posture is not to be stood to attention, but rather being crouched down with their feet on blocks. From my perspective, that has always looked uncomfortable and looks to be more of a hindrance than a help.

I have often thought about this posture when it comes to starting things in my own life. I wonder if, at times, we are too quick to start our race without first adopting the right posture. We can be in such a hurry to get the task started that we can fail to pay attention to the way in which we start. Yet our internal posture will either help or hinder our external race. It's the ability to control the starting process that determines the pace and power of our performance once the starter gun is sounded. In a professional race the smallest error in that starting line up can throw the whole race out. An incorrect starting position can even mean disqualification.

The runners follow a three step command. They are told: "On your marks," then, "Get set," until finally they can, "Go." These are not just words that are recited but instructions to every runner to assume the proper position. How many times do we follow this process, spiritually, before we set off? Do we allow time to get "on our marks" with our feet on the starting blocks, much like bending our knees in prayer? To "get set"—to set our hearts, our thinking and priorities on Christ so that we can run without unnecessary hindrance? And then, with these things in place, we can follow through with the strength and speed we need as we react to the final command—"Go!"

Often, it seems we just want to hear that final command, "Go!" We want the gun to fire and the race to begin. But all of our going, physically, should be springing from a life that has aligned itself spiritually. I recently was launching into a new project and in the haste to get things moving I had started running without taking any time to assess the cost and implications it would have in my world. As I was pushing ahead I felt God whisper into my spirit to stop and slow down because there was a "foot fault." Just as in the race, runners who start incorrectly are called back to the block for "foot faults." I felt God was calling me spiritually back. He was letting me know my start was invalid and if I didn't address it now, I would pay for it later. I hadn't surrendered before I had started. I hadn't prayed before I pursued. Rather than risk disqualification, I decided to back up and start again. This time, rather than jump into things feet first, to adopt a posture that would put me at His feet first.

In Matthew 26:7 we read about the woman who brought the alabaster jar of expensive perfume to Jesus. Scripture records that as she came with her gift to Jesus and poured it out at his feet in worship, she created a moment that Jesus used to teach the disciples of their own "foot fault" in the way they had approached Him that day. Though many were at the house with Jesus, they had not welcomed Jesus. It was this woman's surrender that highlighted the "foot fault" in them, as He reminded them in Luke 7:46, "You did not put oil on my head, but she has poured perfume on my feet." The disciples were preoccupied with what was on the table that day, while this woman only had eyes for who was at the table. She entered the room with a different mindset. She hadn't come to eat a "feast first"; she had come to be at His "feet first."

Even in the busyness of our lives we must always take time to surrender our agendas at His feet and be willing to examine our approach into each situation. When we don't set our focus on the right things, we can end up serving the wrong things. Just as this woman's perfume changed the whole atmosphere in that room, so a life that surrenders before it serves can change entire communities. Let your life have an aroma of surrender. Where do you need to go back to the start and re-align your posture today? Dare to admit if there has been a foot fault and surrender your agenda again at his feet.

YOUR DAILY DARE

1. Is your spiritual posture aligned correctly?

2. What do you need to re-align so you can run with greater strength?

3. What agenda do you need to surrender at His feet first?

dare to be
TRUSTING
by ng

DARE TO BE *TRUSTING*

"'For I know the plans I have for you,' declares the Lord, 'plans to prosper you and not to harm you. Plans to give you hope and a future.'"

Jeremiah 29:11 NIV

I have always felt that music was one of the most powerful mediums for conveying truth, expressing emotion and reaching people in a way nothing else can. This theory was proven to me early on in my career. When I was just venturing into the music world, I was a part of a group called Truth. We played nearly 300 dates a year (yes...300) and traveled all over. One night, though, we were back in Seattle at my home church. My friends and family were in the audience and it was a blessing to perform for them.

Something happened that night, though, that I'll never forget. During one of our songs, "God is in Control," I looked up to see my nine year old nephew standing by himself, hands raised, tears streaming down his face, claiming that truth of the lyrics as his own:

God is in control, though godless men conspire. / His will unfolds though mortal men may always seem to doubt. / His ways are higher than our ways. / So even through the fire, take heart and know God is in control.

My sister later shared with me that her son had said to her, "That song's just for me." At the time, my nephew was facing the greatest tragedy his little heart had known—his parents were getting divorced. My sister also shared that she had recently walked in on him, moaning in anguished sounds that shouldn't have to come from a 9-year old, crying and asking for Daddy. All she could do was scoop him into her arms, hold him and remind him of the powerful message in that song. As he let the peace of the All-Mighty's power wash over him, it was as if God Himself was holding him in His arms.

Truth is, He was. And He does the same for you and me everyday. We all know that life is hard, painful and unjust. Sometimes the circumstances we face make no sense—especially if we are Christians. After all, we've committed our hearts to the Creator of heaven and earth...shouldn't He be able to shield us from some of this pain? Of course, He can. He has every capacity to orchestrate a pain-free life for anyone anywhere anytime. But, He has instead given us free will. And with that will, we have fallen along with our broken world. Tragedy, loss and pain are consequences of our decisions. And their repercussions impact both the innocent and guilty.

And so, while we're not guaranteed an easy or smooth ride through life, we are promised the stronghold of God to never waiver or leave. We are promised that no matter how alone we feel or how deeply we hurt, we can trust that God is still working all things for good. That's what my nephew discovered and claimed as his own that night. Despite the upheaval of his world, he chose to trust God's sovereignty. Despite not understanding the purpose of his circumstances, he chose to trust that God has already worked them through to the end. That's not easy to do. Many times, when dark clouds appear on the horizon, I default to—*OK God, what did I do now to make you so mad at me?* I have a hard time stepping back to see the big picture. I forget that my darkest day is just another thread in His beautiful tapestry that I won't even see on this earth. I lose myself in the darkness around me. Before long, I don't even feel like crawling towards a light.

But that's not God's desire. He knows our hurts. He knows our losses. He knows our doubts. And He *is* trustworthy to redeem, deliver and sanctify.

It's up to us not only to believe that, but to ask for it and expect it. I dare you today to pray for a perspective that is bigger than your circumstances. I dare you to trust that God isn't through with you or your story. I dare you to accept that you do not know the end and REST in the knowledge that He does. Be it a song or scripture or a smile from a stranger, pray that God will show you, today, evidence of His promises fulfilled in your life... and for the many promises to come.

YOUR DAILY DARE

1. What are you having trouble trusting God with today?

2. Do you really believe that your darkest circumstances are part of a greater work?

3. Do you believe that God is working all things for your good?

dare to be PATIENT

by cg

DARE TO BE *PATIENT*

"He has made everything beautiful in its time."
Ecclesiastes 3:11 ESV

In today's fast-paced culture, no one wants to wait. We all seem to be rushing faster and faster so we're not overtaken or left behind. There's not much room for patience in our instant gratification world. And yet, the Bible tells us in Ecclesiastes 3:11 that there is a season for everything. Everything is beautiful in its time. Therefore, patience is something we must dare to embrace.

When I consider my list of virtues, I wouldn't necessarily rank patience very high. It's more like a work in progress. After making the mistake of rushing far too often, I've learned to value the grace of waiting. I can strive in my own strength or work in God's grace. I know which will produce the longest lasting fruit. Much like cause and effect, impatience will produce a result; but it will be no more than a poor substitute for God's timely provision. Impatience prompted Abraham to try to force God's promise, which ultimately resulted in the birth of Ishmael. How often we do the same...creating Ishmael's when we should be waiting for Isaac's.

So why do we do it? Why do we opt for the here and now attitude? Largely because it's easier and seemingly more satisfying—at first... But, every door impatience leads us to force open, becomes another door we have to struggle and fight to keep open in the future. Our restlessness must become anchored in a better understanding of God's timing and perspective, which mandates patience. Patience requires self-control. When you want to run, it tells you to stay. When you want to say, "Bring it on," patience tells you to let others go first. Patience allows for a process to work. It says, "I am not doing this in my own strength."

When my son asks me to come build Legos with him, sometimes I respond immediately, but other times, I let him know that I'll be there as soon as I finish what I'm doing. At this, he responds one of two ways. He either trusts that I am on my way or he can become frustrated by my delay. When I do join him to build Legos, he is sometimes happily playing, awaiting my arrival, with every confidence that I was on my way the whole time. Other times, he has thrown Lego pieces everywhere because he had to wait. As a result of his impatience, the Lego pieces he was so looking forward to sharing with me in the first place are now lost.

Very often, we do the same with God. When we ask Him to come and be a part of our lives, His reply may look different than what we had imagined or hoped for. Sometimes, it's immediate, but other times He simply tells us, "I'm on my way. Wait for me." At that point, do you wait or do you allow impatience to cause you unrest? We have to trust that if God's intervention isn't instant, it doesn't mean that He's not coming. Daring to be patient means to replace nagging with trusting, panic with prayer and frustration with faith.

Once, in John 11, some of Jesus' friends desperately needed a miracle. He told them that He was coming and would heal their brother, Lazarus. But Jesus didn't come immediately. In fact, Lazarus died. Everyone involved was devastated and confused. It seemed as though Jesus had failed them. But, Jesus said He would come. He just didn't say when. When He does arrive, He calls forth Lazarus from the dead and reunites the grieving family. He shows that even when God's delay means death, it has no power over the carrier of eternal life. We must have the courage to embrace God's timing even when we don't understand it.

Today, as you go about your day, I dare you to be patient. Resist the urge to try to make it happen on your own. Wait on the One who makes everything beautiful in its time.

YOUR DAILY DARE

1. Where do you need to be more patient?

2. Today, what is it that you can stop forcing and begin entrusting to God?

3. What door has your impatience closed that you need to be willing to open again?

dare to be STILL

by *ng*

DARE TO BE *STILL*

"But Martha was distracted by all the preparations that had to be made. She came to him and asked, 'Lord, don't you care that my sister has left me to do the work by myself? Tell her to help me!' 'Martha, Martha,' the Lord answered, 'You are worried and upset about many things, but few things are needed—or indeed only one. Mary has chosen what is better, and it will not be taken away from her.'"

Luke 10:40-42

This passage has always bothered me a little. Probably because I identify much more strongly with Martha than Mary...I am GREAT at staying busy. Give me a to-do list and I'm a happy girl. I like knowing that I'm needed and am meeting a need, serving a desire or contributing something tangible. All those Type A gals out there know where I'm coming from. There's a certain exhilaration that emerges when we look around at all the plates we're spinning...especially when we're spinning more than everyone else.

In a way, I get it honest. I have an extraordinary family, who all seem to excel at everything they do. And while there wasn't a spoken expectation or pressure to fall in step and be the absolute best in everything...or at least to DO everything...I so wanted to please my family and everyone else, that I let busyness creep into my persona to the point where I hardly even acknowledged it or thought twice about it. I just did everything. That's who I was. I found energy and direction in my endless tasks.

But ask me to sit still? To rest? Nooooooo! When I'm still, I can see things and hear things that I'd rather not. When at rest, my own heart and hurts and fears come out to play. And, pesky things, they vie convincingly for my attention. What I see, I don't always like. More than that, when I really see myself—not my tasks—I have to entertain the notion that other people may be seeing this less-than-wonderful person as well. When I'm busy, I'm numb to that. And God knows it. God can see that I'm deriving my worth, many times, from my accomplishments. God knows that the more I do, the more self-sufficient I think I am...making me less dependent on Him.

I think that's what God was getting at through this passage. Both sisters were focused. Both sisters were attentive and intentional. But only one had her attention fixed on the right subject. While Martha was busy being busy, Mary was at the feet of her Lord—learning, listening, growing. To be honest, there's still a part of me that feels Martha's indignation. After all, people needed to eat and a clean house to stay in... She was making it all happen. And if I were flitting around while my sister sat doing (apparently) nothing, I'd probably want someone to say something on my behalf too.

But here we see, perhaps as clearly as anywhere else in scripture, how very different God's priorities are from our own. His priority isn't what we produce or accomplish. He's much more interested in the time we spend getting to know Him. Because to know Him is to love Him. God wants our love...not our lists. He wants us to experience every bit of life—joy, pain, loss, victory—in its fullness; not as a numb afterthought.

As I'm writing these words, I do so with trepidation because this is not something that I have mastered. I'm still much more comfortable being busy. And I'm still afraid sometimes to sit still long enough to see all of me... But that's when I try to remember Mary. God didn't think she was lazy or unaccomplished. He knew that in her stillness, she was loving Him. And despite her best intentions, Martha was too busy to focus on her Lord.

What about you? Is it easier, more comfortable for you to stay busy? Does being still make you nervous? I dare you to create a time—yes, actually schedule it—to be still. Cancel your appointments or obligations for an hour a week (for starters)...pick a quiet spot, turn off your phone and just be with your Lord. It may feel awkward or make you uneasy, but the rewards will be great. I dare you to lay down your Martha. Take up your Mary.

YOUR DAILY DARE

1. Do you stay busy for the sake of staying busy?

2. When is the last time you took a long look at the woman in the mirror? How well do you know her?

3. Do you trust God with the time you give Him?

dare to be
CONSISTENT

by CG

DARE TO BE *CONSISTENT*

"Jesus Christ is the same yesterday and today and forever!"

Hebrews 13:8 NIV

I will never forget one evening, as a recently married couple, we had invited some friends over for dinner to our new home. I have never been a great chef, but there are a few dishes I can cook, so I chose to play it safe and make one of my favorite foolproof lasagnas. When the time came to serve the food, I remember sinking the knife into the lasagna dish, only to find that there was nothing to cut through! The dish was more like a meat soup, so I scooped it from dish to plate with a ladle! I couldn't understand what had happened. I had made this dish before on several occasions, yet it was all wrong. But, as we had hungry guests, I served the lasagna in bowls!

That night as I lay in bed still wondering why my culinary disaster had occurred, I suddenly realized "lasagna sheets!" I had forgotten to add the lasagna sheets to my dish! I had been so busy layering on the sauce and the cheese that I forgot the most important ingredient—the part that holds it all together. While this may not have huge and lasting consequences in regards to my lasagna, the truth is if we are not careful we can build our lives with that same inconsistency. We can layer our lives without the spiritual "sheets" that hold it all together.

As a working mom, wife, leader and friend there can be so many layers in life to manage. Add to that the ever-changing inconsistent world we live in and it can sometimes seem that daily circumstances are changing and altering our course. Therefore, it becomes vitally important that we add disciplines to our lives that create the same effect as those lasagna sheets—consistent behavior that hold us up in the inconsistent circumstances.

So what are some of the layers we could add to our lives? It will be different for each of us, but here are a few I can wholeheartedly recommend. How about adding the layer of consistency that comes from the word of God and prayer? Not just opening a bible on Sunday or praying when facing a crisis, but because we are committing to having that layer binding all of life's decisions and activities...

Or what about the layers of generosity? I remember as a young girl deciding I wanted to be someone who sowed financial seed; not because I was made to, but because I wanted to plant seed in the ground for my future. I took my first paycheck at 15 years old and gave some of it away. It wasn't much in amount, but it was a huge step in my commitment to begin to add a layer of generosity into my everyday life. The truth is there is no such thing as a spontaneous harvest. Ask any farmer and they will tell you the only way to guarantee a harvest is to sow seed consistently. A life that is committed to being generous doesn't let the economy or circumstances determine its sowing schedule. It commits to add the consistency of generosity, which holds firm in every changing economic climate.

In Psalm 92:13 God gives us another consistent layer to build on, He tells us that "planted in the house of God we will flourish." Planting is an act of permanence. I have been in the same church for over 30 years and there have been times I have felt like uprooting. It's not always easy to consistently commit. But when you do, that commitment becomes a source of strength to your life. I am so glad I decided to add a layer of commitment, which pushed past the temporary pain so I could inherit the eternal rewards of a flourishing life that consistency has brought.

Inconsistency will eventually undo what you begin. Like the man who built his house upon the sand, an inconsistent foundation will not keep your house steady when the storms come. It's the disciplines that we commit to add that will keep us strong. It's the core values that will help our commitment in a season of challenge. Don't let your life be built on shifting sand; rather, add foundational layers of consistency.

Maybe the thing you need is not another adventure, opportunity, friendship or provision. Maybe it's something far less exciting and much more basic. Maybe the answer to this season of your life is to go back and add those consistent commitments, the spiritual "sheets" that will bring cohesion. We serve a God who is the same, yesterday, today and forever, I would say that was pretty consistent wouldn't you? I dare you to follow His example today as you dare to be consistent.

YOUR DAILY DARE

1. Where are there inconsistencies in your life?

2. What daily discipline can you add to bring some stability and cohesion?

3. What commitment can you make today to increase your consistency as a person?

dare to be BROKEN

by ng

DARE TO BE *BROKEN*

"My sacrifice, O God, is a broken spirit; a broken and contrite heart you, God, will not despise."
Psalm 51:17 NIV

Most children aspire to greatness. They envision themselves as heroes with lots of money and friends and romance. (At least I did). When you ask a kid what he or she wants to be when they grow up, odds are not high that the answer will be, "Broken." No one wants to break. No one wants to be weak—especially in today's culture! Our endless pursuit of self-reliance and ambition has conditioned us not only to prefer strength, but to find anything less than unappealing and certainly nothing to aim for.

The church is quite possibly one of the biggest hotbeds for the perpetuation of the Super-Christian, Super-Human ideal. After all, we have Christ in our hearts...so we should be good with everything, right? Not only are we to be happy and on good behavior; we're expected to have clean children in adorable clothes, perfectly coiffed hair with no fly-aways and an impeccably clean car always primed for a car pool. My, are our standards high! The ridiculous thing is...as much as we know that our ideals are ridiculous...we move heaven and earth to at least appear to uphold them. We know we shouldn't really care about how we look, how we come across or how we're perceived, but we do. A lot.

I'm one of the best at maintaining a saccharin-sweet façade. I know the expectations of the rest of the world—especially my family's and my church's—and I know how to meet and exceed them. I know how to conceal my own heartache or mistake or disillusionment with life. Sometimes I feel like I wrote the manual on maintaining your mask. The problem is, it's not true. The façade...the perfection...it's all a lie. Not that you or I intentionally deceive those around us or even ourselves; we've just become so conditioned to upholding the ruse, we barely even think about it anymore.

Moment of truth...God thinks about it. God thinks about you and me and our masks and our secrets and our hurts and our longings that otherwise go unspoken. God thinks about our brokenness. If He didn't He wouldn't have sent His only son to suffer because of our fragility. The church is full of broken people. How do I know? Because the church is full of people. It's intrinsic for us to not be able to do life alone. We are innately incapable of making our way through the day to day by ourselves. And that's OK! It's the lack of our capability that will one day send us to our knees...or knock us flat on our faces.

It took me a long time to learn this lesson because it required me to reconcile the knowledge of my own depravity juxtaposed with the excessive grace of God that, for all intents and purposes, makes no sense whatsoever. I was so good at upholding my good Christian mask, I didn't realize that the secrets I was keeping from the rest of the world were slowly eating me alive. While I convinced others that I was this flawless creature, I began to expect it to be true. And, while it wasn't and never could be, I became increasingly disillusioned and disappointed with myself.

It's the perfect storm, really... We think we should wear a mask to conceal our brokenness; the mask becomes a part of our psyche and we spiral further into self-loathing; our spiral and the desperate attempt to keep up appearances makes us distance ourselves from others who might see the truth. Thus, we end up alone, confused and even more broken than when we began. Despite it all, however, God doesn't look at us and see a crumpled heap of jagged edges, comprising the shattered pieces of our lives. He sees a child whom He has redeemed.

It's up to us to step out in faith and trust that God's perspective is much more in line with reality than our own. It's up to us to trust that even in our depravity, God sees us, wants us and loves us. I dare you today to acknowledge the brokenness in your life. As you do, I dare you to share those dark places with God, trusting His healing hand. And, I dare you to come clean with the rest of the world. Keeping your façade in check is hard, draining work. And it saps our energy that could be/should be directed at something that truly matters. Pray to see the healing and beauty that awaits you in the brokenness. Claim for yourself the promise that God isn't finished with you...and He desires ALL of your pieces to come before His loving throne. For it's when we're broken that the potter can begin to put our pieces back together once again.

YOUR DAILY DARE

1. What mask are you wearing at church? At work? At home?

2. What are you afraid of discovering if you acknowledge your brokenness?

3. Do you trust that God can make something beautiful from your broken pieces?

Day 8

dare to be BEAUTIFUL

by cg

DARE TO BE *BEAUTIFUL*

"Cultivate inner beauty, the gentle, gracious kind that God delights in."

1 Peter 3:4 MSG

We have all had those days when we wake up, look in the mirror and see that unwanted blemish that has emerged overnight in the most annoying of places. At the sight of this "ugly" we usually do one of two things—either cover it up with foundation and concealer or squeeze it in the hopes it will go away.

In much the same way, the enemy will seek to put an "ugly" on the beauty of your life in Christ. He specializes in placing irritation under your skin, trying to create a blemish of bitterness and scars from jealously and envy. We have to commit to become women who don't try to hide or cover over these "uglies," but rather to let God's word and love cleanse them, thereby restoring us.

In Genesis 29, we meet two sisters who both had their own blemishes with which to contend. The older sister, Leah, was told from an early age she was not beautiful. She was described as "dull in appearance" and compared constantly to her beautiful, younger sister, Rachel. Leah's father, believing she wasn't lovely enough to find love on her own, even tricked Jacob, her sister's suitor, by disguising Leah as his bride. No wonder Leah found it hard to believe that there was any beauty in her life! Yet Leah's story goes on to show us how she was able to move from a place of rejection to a place of rejoicing.

After separating from those around her, Leah dared to trust God by opening her heart again and letting Him love her. God's love looks for those who feel unlovely, desiring to make them beautiful again. Gen 29 says, "God loved Leah and He opened her womb." She became pregnant and went on to have three more children, who all became part of her healing process. Leah gave each child a name that marked the journey God had taken her on from brokenness to beauty, from barrenness and bitterness, to having a new life and hope in Him. Let's learn from her journey how we too can dare to be beautiful again.

Leah named her first-born Reuben, which means "God sees." When we have blemishes in our life, we can feel no one would want to look at us, so we hide and become isolated. Leah had been overlooked all her life, told she was ugly and hidden from sight. But this first child awakened her to the knowledge that God had seen, valued and loved her just as she was.

Her second son she named Simeon, which means "God hears." The "uglies" in life can often silence us. We become embarrassed, even fearful to speak up, so we stay quiet. Leah had to learn that she had a voice...and God had heard it.

Her third child was named Levi, whose name means "companionship." I love this part of Leah's restoration. Leah had never felt worthy of companionship—not from her sister, father or her husband. She had felt unworthy of being loved by someone, but when Levi was born, through the gift of this third son, she knew God was her greatest companion.

Her fourth son was Judah, whose name means "praise God." Through the process of allowing God to bring out beauty in her life, Leah understood God saw and heard her. He had chosen to be her companion and loved her and she was able to move her life from a place of pain, to a posture of praise.

When we become scarred by the "uglies" and insecurities of life, we also have to be willing to embark on a journey. We have to be brave enough to open our lives again to let God reveal the beauty that is within. Thankfully, we don't have to get physically pregnant to take this journey! But we do have to be spiritually open to find that God sees, hears and wants to be our greatest companion. You have to dare to be the beauty He made you to be.

YOUR DAILY DARE

1. What are you covering that needs His light to shine on it?

2. Where have you believed you are ugly when God calls you beautiful?

3. What can you do today to open up and let the healing begin?

dare to be KNOWN

by ng

DARE TO BE *KNOWN*

"Jesus said to her, 'You are right when you say you have no husband. The fact is, you have had five husbands, and the man you now have is not your husband. What you have just said is quite true.'"

John 4:17 NIV

Do you remember when you first discovered Facebook? How about Twitter? Did you jump on the bandwagon immediately? Or, like me, did it take some getting used to the fact that nearly everyone you've ever met and many people you haven't now have a glimpse into your life any hour of the day, every single day of the year? In a very loose sense, Facebook keeps us all on a kind of constant surveillance from friends, family and (as much as we would like to think otherwise) our bosses, professional colleagues and fellow church goers.

Without question, people know more about other people today than ever before. And all evidence shows that we love it! What's more exciting than posting new pix of the party last weekend or your baby's first steps? What better way is there to stay connected to people who love "Grey's Anatomy," "Dancing with the Stars" or other such guilty pleasures as much as you do than through fan pages? And, go on, admit it...it's still pretty exciting when someone requests to be our friend or starts following us on Twitter or even endorses us on Linkedin. There's a certain exhilaration and reward that comes when more and more people get to know us. At long last, our popularity can be monitored, quantified and strategized. The more likes we have, the better we're doing, right?

Right...with one caveat. As long as we get to control the amount and type of information that is circulating in the cosmos about ourselves, we're good with it. It's great for lots and lots of people to know just a little about us. But what about letting them know more? What about letting anyone know more? Suddenly, being known isn't quite as exciting. It's actually a little disconcerting. I know I certainly don't want everyone knowing everything about me. There are certain pieces of my life that I don't want anyone to know about me. Ever.

I have a feeling that's how the Samaritan woman at the well felt. Actually, I'm pretty positive that she knew exactly what it's like to try to hide parts of your life...or your entire life from others. She was going to the well at the hottest part of the day. Why? She knew that was the time of day that she was least likely to run into anyone else. This woman had a past. Her present was spotty and her track record overall wasn't exactly virtuous. She wasn't proud of it, but she had learned to navigate her community in order to maintain it. She knew the paths to walk and how to time her day so as not to meet any questioning eyes or be confronted with her own shame. She knew how to remain comfortably unknown.

She just hadn't counted on the one who knew her more intimately than she knew herself to be waiting at the well. Her initial shock came at the prospect of a Jewish man who would speak to a Samaritan woman. That was soon outweighed by what He said. By what He knew. Her past, her secrets, her shame...He knew it all. And much to her surprise, He didn't judge her. In fact, He not only spoke to her; He asked her for water—yet another cultural taboo. And then, He told her about living water and how He was the Messiah. So excited and in awe of this man, the woman ran into the town—yes, the one she very intentionally avoided in her day to day—to tell them of this man she had met who had told her about everything she'd ever done. So touched by Jesus' response to her, despite every mistake and wrong decision she'd ever made, she was compelled to share Him with others. In a sense, His utter acceptance of her prompted her to share a piece of her heart with those she had feared.

How often do we let our fear of what others might think or assume about us predicate our own avoidance techniques? Why do we just assume that no one will love us or like us or stay with us if they knew the truth? And then, why do we fear that the reaction of others will be worse than the work of maintaining our façade? I dare you to move beyond accumulating shallow acquaintances and invest in some deep relationships. I dare you to be honest with yourself, with God and with at least one other person about who you are. I dare you to be known.

YOUR DAILY DARE

1. Do you place more of a priority on "knowing" people than letting people really know you?

2. What in your life are you afraid to reveal to others?

3. What does it mean to you to realize that God does know EVERYTHING about you...and still loves you beyond reason? Carry that with you everyday.

dare to be CHANGED

by cg

DARE TO BE *CHANGED*

"Anyone who listens to the Word but does not do what it says is like someone who looks at his face in a mirror and, after looking at himself, goes away and immediately forgets what he looks like."

James 1:23, 24 NIV

Change is a consistent part of all of our lives. We may not like, want or think we need it, but change will and does happen to us all. So the question we have to answer is: will we avoid or embrace it? I have never been great with change. I don't mind it happening around me as much as I mind when it has to happen in me. I have learned to dare to become more changeable, and by doing so, I have lessened the pain of this regular visitor in my life.

We can be like James 1:23 with change—seeing the need for it but then walking away unsure of how to make it happen. Yet, we have to be willing to acknowledge that change is a consistent mark of a growing life. We may want to avoid it, but we're really just stockpiling change for a later date.

I remember one time struggling with a change I needed to make. I handled a situation badly and my pride and stubbornness convinced me to leave it alone. Weeks went by and with the delay the enemy added interest to the problem. My hesitancy to change almost caused permanent damage. That's why I know that even though we don't like it, we have to dare to change.

The problem can often lie in our lack of understanding of how to change and so we need to simplify the procedure in our life. Let's consider approaching change as if we are going into a changing room at a store—an image most of us can appreciate. When we enter a department store changing room, there is an expected behavior we have to adhere to.

Spiritually, there is also changing room etiquette we need to learn if we want to do change well.

Changing rooms have an item restriction policy. They don't let you try on the whole store at one time. The same principal must be applied spiritually. If we attempt too many changes at once, we will tire and end up changing nothing. Instead, make regular changes. 2 Corinthians 13:5 says to "examine your life," checking if there are any areas to adjust. Frequently entering into God's great changing room reduces the risk of it becoming an overwhelming changing room disaster.

In order to change, we also have to be willing to take things off. If we want to wear what's new, we have to remove what's old and worn out. It sounds obvious, but so often we want to try to keep what is old while putting on what is new. But change requires an exchange. Something has to be removed, to be replaced. Isaiah 61:3 says to take gladness instead of mourning and take beauty for ashes. It doesn't say take gladness "as well as" mourning, to take beauty "as well as" ashes, but to take them instead of. You need to be willing to remove the old for the new. Stop multi-layering and start changing.

All great changing rooms have trained assistants, and God's is no exception. When God asked Moses to bring change, He let him take his brother Aaron with him. Although Moses could have gone in God's strength alone to Pharaoh, God in His grace knew he needed this changing assistant. Ruth entered her next season of change with an older and wiser "Naomi" at her side. David had Jonathan, who helped him navigate Saul's leadership. Jonathan became David's friend as David brought change that affected an entire nation. God will also give us changing assistance, sometimes in a friend, other times in a book or advice from someone who has journeyed the change before you. The Holy Spirit is always on hand as our ultimate change assistant, but we have to be willing to accept the help He gives.

Just as you can't live in a store's changing room, the same is true in God's. Don't let your reluctance to change prolong the process, or allow endless hesitation to hold up the change that will enhance your future. God wants change to become part of our way of life. We need to dare to be changeable and dare to let our hearts be regularly examined. The good news is, change happens to us all. No one gets to avoid change. You are not alone. Enjoy the process, rather than endure it. Dare to be changed today.

YOUR DAILY DARE

1. What change are you avoiding?

2. Where are you trying to change too many things at once?

3. What assistance do you need to accept in your change?

dare to be GENEROUS

by ng

DARE TO BE *GENEROUS*

"Jesus sat down opposite the place where the offerings were put and watched the crowd putting their money into the temple treasury. Many rich people threw in large amounts. But a poor widow came and put in two very small copper coins, worth only a fraction of a penny. Calling His disciples to Him, Jesus said, 'I tell you the truth, this poor widow has put more into the treasury than all the others. They all gave out of their wealth; but she, out of her poverty, put in everything—all she had to live on.'"

Mark 12:41-44 NIV 1984

The last several years have been unprecedented when it comes to human tragedy. From September 11 to tsunamis and earthquakes to hurricanes and war, people all over the world have endured horrendous conditions. Add to it an economy that has been, at best, unstable and, at worst, teetering on the edge of another great depression. Times have been tough. Despite the losses, however, people have come forward to help. Donations have been given, relief workers have been sent, heroes have emerged. In the throes of loss, generosity has poured forth. And thanks to technology, it's become increasingly convenient to give. A quick text to the Red Cross, and you've sent your ten dollars overseas. A click of a mouse and that shoebox is stuffed and sent around the world. And hear me when I say... these are all good things.

But what happens when the tragedies subside? What happens when the day to day resumes? Do you avert your eyes from the homeless man holding a sign? Do you dig through your purse, looking busy, waiting for the deacon and his offering plate to pass you by? What about your son or daughter who asks for your time and attention when you get home? Or your parent who merely wants a phone call? What happens once generosity is no longer convenient or popular?

In the gospels of Mark and Luke, we read the tale of the widow who gave two mites. Most of us know the story. While others were giving larger sums of money, she threw in the last two coins to her name. In and of themselves, they were practically worthless...worth less than pennies in today's currency. On almost any other day, she and her donation would probably have gone completely unnoticed. But not that day.

Jesus noticed.

He noticed that out of all the money being given that day, that none gave so much as this woman. He knew that she had just given her entire livelihood. Despite having practically nothing, she chose to be generous. That wasn't convenient or popular or even advisable by the world's standards. But in terms of the divine, she could not have more purely demonstrated her understanding of her Savior and His heart. Her own generosity mirrored that of Jesus'. Throughout His 33 years on this earth, He lived generously. He gave of His time. He gave of His power. He gave of His unwavering love for us. Much like the widow, He wasn't a man of great resources when it came to material wealth. And yet over and over, we read that He who had nothing...she who had nothing...gave the most.

That is the kind of generosity I dare you to pursue. I dare you to give more than you feel comfortable. I dare you to give more than you think you can. Be it your money or time or love, I dare you to be lavish just as the Heavenly Father lavished redemption on the world through the sacrifice of His son. Tragedies will always exist. There will always be a relief effort in need of money and skill. And we should all continuously be mindful of and responsive to them. But don't stop there. Don't wait for a tragedy to prompt your heart. And don't separate the rest of your life from your giving. Within your family, your work place, your church, live with your hands and heart open. Pray for opportunities to give of yourself. When those opportunities emerge, don't hold back. Dare yourself to be radically generous...not conveniently so.

Every life touched by tragedy around the world is in need of someone's selflessness. The same holds true for your family and community. Never underestimate the degree to which you are needed. And never doubt the blessings you in turn will receive. Even if no one is around...much like the widow, Jesus sees your heart. He sees what you give and what you withhold. He notices you. So, as the giver of all life and love has done, let your generosity be extravagant. Let your love be lavish...and let your life reflect the One who gave all.

YOUR DAILY DARE

1. What am I withholding from God?

2. How am I allocating my resources?

3. How can I move beyond safety to the uncomfortable, unrestrained love the Father has given to me?

dare to be HONEST

by cg

DARE TO BE *HONEST*

"The old has passed away; behold, the new has come."

2 Cor 5:17 ESV

When I was younger, I recall hanging out at my friend's house when for some inexplicable reason a friend decided that she would try to perform a cartwheel in the rather small lounge we were sitting in. What began as a graceful piece of gymnastics ended up as an expensive disaster! Her right foot kicked the family's prize crystal fruit bowl into the air and consequently into a thousand tiny pieces of broken glass. This then led to several hours of panic and futile activity as we tried to Scotch tape the bowl back together piece by piece before my friend's mom returned home from the store.

Scotch tape was never going to work, but faced with the option of either being honest to my friend's mother about her prized bowl or taping it together, the tape somehow seemed the more appealing choice. We managed to get the bowl to a place where one side was held together by tape that was hidden and positioned out of view, in the hope that no one would notice. Our plan worked for a while, until the mother brought in a bag of apples to place in the fruit bowl. As she emptied out the apples, the inevitable took place. The tape gave way under the weight and our deceit was made apparent.

When I think back to that glass bowl, it seemed such a ridiculous way to spend three hours. Too often we would rather spend many hours trying to tape together the shards of brokenness in our own lives rather than facing the truth. We don't want to own up to the embarrassment of being honest or the vulnerability it creates. Instead we look for ways to cover the struggle. Too often we would rather tape up our marriage than admit it's broken. We tape up our hurts, we cover over our sin and failures and every time we apply the tape we delay the healing process. Consequently when we do try to grow or God adds to our life, just like that glass bowl, the increase adds pressure until eventually what we are trying to hold together gives way, and all that we were called to carry becomes damaged in the process.

Remember when King David sinned with Bathsheba? This mistake was bad enough, but it was the behavior that followed that made the situation worse. If he had been honest about his sin with Bathsheba when it happened, then the situation would have been dealt with and the process of restoration could have begun. However, David chose instead to conceal and hide his sin; he let his pride and power take matters into his own hands.

David began to tape the situation up hoping to conceal his actions, which soon led to more dishonesty. He had Bathsheba's husband murdered, lied to his most trusted staff and his sin led to the death of the child he had conceived with Bathsheba. Despite David's legacy being tarnished, he still didn't want anyone to see the cracks in his life. The beginning of all healing is always honesty and until David was honest, his life continued to create collateral damage.

Fear of what others will think can prompt us to get the tape out in our lives. We don't want to be embarrassed; we don't want to be ridiculed. Guilt and fear can stop us from daring to be honest and will imprison us in brokenness and shame. We must dare to be honest, face the fear and trust our awesome God. God doesn't just tape over our cracks but can "make all things new" (2 Corinthians 5:17).

Don't be fooled into thinking you can hold it all together. Only God can do that. Maybe it is time to stop taping and start talking to God. Let's get honest and ask where we need to let the panic subside and the pride fall away. Where do we need to admit truth and speak up about how we are really doing? The reality is, God knows and sees everything and He still loves you completely. So why keep pretending? God is not looking to humiliate or expose you, He wants to heal and make you whole. So stop taping today and dare to be honest.

YOUR DAILY DARE

1. What have you taped together that you need to let God heal?

2. Where has fear created a prison that honesty can unlock?

3. Pray today for the courage to stop taping and start talking.

dare to be

HELD

by ng

DARE TO BE *HELD*

"He will carry the lambs in His arms, holding them close to His heart."
Isaiah 40:11 NLT

As a new mom, I remember watching my twin babies sleep, dreaming of the day they would reach their arms to me and ask me to hold them. They were so tiny and frail, and I just knew the magical day would come when they would call my name and ask for my arms. That moment is forever cemented in my mind. As they were just becoming toddlers, I will never forget walking in to the nursery, seeing Gracie standing in her crib with her arms extended, "Up momma, up." Bella soon followed, only hers came out as "Pup momma, pup." To my mommy ears, sweeter words had never been spoken! Then my youngest Sadie came along. When she discovered her voice, she delivered "up momma" with a demanding shout! And with pleasure, I bent down, scooped her up and cradled her in my arms.

Every child longs to be held, and as a mother, one of the strongest desires I have is to wrap my arms around my children. What a treasure to discover that this is exactly the same desire my heavenly Father has for me. When I came across Isaiah 40:1, I loved the picture it created in my mind, that God scoops me up like a little lamb, and carries me close to his heart. We all have a desire to be held, one that can only ever be fully met in the Everlasting Arms.

Several years ago, I had the privilege of recording a song called "Held." Written by Christa Wells, this song was born out of great loss. Christa had watched some of her dear friends suffer through the death of their 2-month old son. Honored to lend my voice to Christa's brilliant lyric and melody, the song was sent out to radio and became one of my biggest hits. I think one of the reasons the song enjoyed such great success, is because so many people resonated with the message. I heard from so many of you who had experienced the death of a loved one, the death of your marriage, or a great loss of some kind. It was almost as if the words in the song reminded people that they aren't walking through their tragedy alone... something all too easy to forget.

I once heard the story of a young girl whose father was tragically killed in a motorcycle accident while he was on his way to see her. For months, she carried guilt around for all of the imagined "what ifs" that torment those who have suffered loss. "What if I had picked up the phone when he called..." "What if I had been kinder and more loving the last time I saw him..." "What if I hadn't invited him down to see me..." The what if spiral is a lonely place to be. And perhaps one of the most difficult is, "What if I could just hold them one more time..."

But the truth is, reaching our hungry arms out into the world, trying to grasp the fact that they won't ever feel that person again, is all at once one of the greatest tests of faith and one of the greatest blessings to cherish. Because while that loved one can no longer be in your arms, he or she is in the eternal arms of the Father. It's as if God entrusted you to hold His baby, His child for a while...and now it's time to give them back.

When you're walking that road of loss, all of the imagery of your father, mother, son, daughter, friend, wife, husband looking down on you from up on high with Jesus isn't always much of a comfort. Those thoughts, much like the words of those who try to comfort in those unspeakable times, don't always mean very much. What we say and hear often feels very fragile against an enemy like sorrow. And even in despair, be it pride or fear or anger, many things make us want to close out the rest of the world. We don't want to be reached by something we don't think will take any of the pain away.

God knows that. And that's OK. That's what His arms are for. Psalms 18:16 says that He reaches down from on high to pull us out of deep waters. In the times when there are no words; in the times when nothing makes sense; and in the times when everything hurts, we have a great promise that He is crying every tear with us and He feels each ragged breath our beaten spirits and hearts take. In those moments, He is the only thing that will help. He is the answer.

If you're hurting, I dare you to let go of all that you're holding inside. For a moment, forget about being strong. I dare you to be held in the arms of your Abba...your daddy. In the one who knew you before you were born, who knows your every heartbeat, rest. Rest and be held by your King.

YOUR DAILY DARE

1. Are you dealing with unresolved grief or loss?

2. Do you find it difficult to admit your hurt or pain to others?

3. Do you trust that, even when you feel alone, that God's arms are holding you? Pray for that feeling to become real for you.

Day 14

dare to

LET IT GO

by cg

DARE TO *LET IT GO*

"A brother offended is more unyielding than a strong city."
Proverbs 18:19 ESV

At some point in time, we all have the opportunity to be offended. We each have had those moments when people have either mistreated or misunderstood us. In those moments we have to decide: do we take the offense, or do we choose to let it go? I have done both, and I can tell you first hand that if you do "take an offense" it will eventually "take from you." It will take your time, your emotions and peace. So today, I want to dare you to let it go.

One of the most startling stories in the Bible reveals just how dangerous carrying offenses can become. In Mark 6:14-29 we read the account of how John the Baptist came to be beheaded. This incredible disciple had his life taken from him because a well-connected woman took an offense. Herodias was Herod's wife, and John had questioned their marriage since it was an unlawful union. When Herodias heard John's comments, she became incensed. It says Herodias "nursed a grudge against John and she wanted him dead" (Mark 6:19).

Have you ever felt that way? I pray we are never as extreme as wanting someone dead, but the truth is, we can get so upset by another's judgment of our situation that we lose all perspective and want to settle the matter, often with no regard for the consequences this could bring.

It states that Herodias "nursed a grudge." This is such a powerful picture of how offenses can attach to our lives. We typically associate the word "nurse" with a mother feeding her newborn baby. When we decide to pick up an offense, we too are beginning to feed that grudge in our lives; we begin to let it attach and gain strength to grow. Herodias nursed her grudge for so long that later in the story, we find her whole family had become affected by it. Even though the offense was not theirs to take, it took over all of their lives, to the point where when Herodias' daughter is extended an opportunity that could change her life forever; she chooses to squander it by exacting her mother's revenge. This young girl ends up with the head of John the Baptist on a platter when she could have inherited up to half of the kingdom in which she lived.

Too many times, when we don't deal with our offenses, they not only deal with us, but all those who are attached to our life. This is especially true for us as women since we are such great connectors. We don't tend to do life alone. We have circles of friendships: from the moms at the schoolyard, to our group of girlfriends, to family and colleagues. When it comes to being offended, it's our ability to live connected that can also be our downfall if we allow the grudge to travel with us. We have the potential to take it a long way in a short space of time. If we let it take center stage in the many conversations in which we are involved over days and weeks, with each person we share, our grudge grows stronger and stronger.

I remember once being offended and letting this offense begin to feed off my life. I would mention my offense on a regular basis and even search for others who would agree with my right to carry this grudge. It wasn't until one day I heard my daughter repeat my offense that I realized this had gone too far. My offense had grown into a full-blown grudge and now innocent people attached to my journey were somehow trying to help me carry it. That day I decided as a mother, friend and wife, that I needed to stop carrying offenses and instead use the strength I had to show that grudge the door.

Your life is too valuable to waste on being bitter. So today, decide to be better. Let God's love heal you, let His forgiveness free you and embrace the peace that comes from letting it go. Choose to feed those things that give you life instead of those that take it from you. Dare to let it go, however hard it may seem. And when you do, you will not only let it go but you will also let your future grow.

YOUR DAILY DARE

1. What offense are you carrying that you need to let go of?

2. Who can you forgive today so that you can be free?

3. What can you stop nursing and feeding? Starve that grudge today.

dare to be UNMASKED

by ng

DARE TO BE *UNMASKED*

"But now, O Lord, you are our Father; we are the clay, and you are our potter; we are all the work of your hand."

Isaiah 64:8 ESV

I have a pretty remarkable family. Growing up, my oldest sister was a scholar, my other sister was beautiful—perfect hair, perfect boyfriend (now perfect husband). Everything my brother touched turned to gold and my third sister was popular, sweet...the one every girl wanted to be and every guy wanted to date. And then there was me. Needless to say, the bar was set pretty high. I lived in fear that I just might be the only underachiever in our family.

Soon enough, my drive for approval and attention underscored everything that I did...not that I didn't get those things readily. My parents believed in me. They continually told me that my potential was limitless. Their confidence in me very soon superceded my own. Because with great expectation comes the potential for great failure. I made a decision early in life to not ever let that happen—despite any cost or sacrifice along the way. I was special. I did have it together. At least that's what the image I was constructing said. In my singularly focused pursuit of achievement, I didn't even entertain self-doubt or the possibility that I might miss the mark. I would NOT disappoint my amazing, loving family.

And as far as anyone else could see, I didn't. But in the quiet darkness of my heart, I knew that the girl everyone else saw wasn't real—not entirely, anyway. Behind that mask of confidence, I was insecure and coming undone on the inside. My quest for perfection had clouded my vision and my heart and it nearly destroyed my health. If perfection included everything (as I had so defined it), then my appearance was on the list too. My strategy of choice was bulimia. In the midst of desperately working towards ridiculous expectations I had put on myself, I used bulimia to cope.

If you've never had an eating disorder, the thought of starving or purging probably seems repulsive. But for me, it was calming, reassuring and, in a way, became something I "needed." Not to mention, if I were to maintain my perfect façade, bulimia was doing the job in the looks department. One small problem with all of this though—I was leading a double life. On one hand, I was ministering, using my gifts, living up to all my family had ever dreamed for me to do. On the other, I was kneeling on cold tile floors, "cleansing" myself, so to speak. I had found a way to maintain every standard...but I had never evaluated the cost of doing so.

Eating disorders demand a certain level of secrecy and denial. They demand acceptance of the idea that who you were created to be is not enough...that you must change to be accepted or loved. This mindset flies in the face of faith. It says that God...the potter...messed up on you. And now, you must fix His mistakes. Without even realizing it, I was becoming lord of my own life. I had constructed the mask and I was keeping it on. And in the process, I was distancing myself from authenticity. Not only did I not allow anyone else to see the real me; I was having an increasingly hard time seeing myself at all. Soon I didn't know where I ended and the mask began...and vice versa.

Eventually, one day, while curled around the base of the toilet, God somehow showed me that this was not the life He had intended for me. I began to see that even though I didn't know who I was...I couldn't be my eating disorder anymore. That was the day I began removing the mask. Not all at once. Not perfectly. Not painlessly. But with an inexplicable feeling that I couldn't go back to the way things had been.

In our culture today, especially among women, it's popular and expected to have it all together and keep it all together. No one applauds a mess. And yet the longer we hide the hurt inside, behind our masks of attempted perfection, the more insidious and devastating the hurt becomes. Soon, we can do little more than ignore it or numb it.

God didn't create us for masks. He created you and me exactly the way He intended...not as something that should be hidden or modified. So if the pressure in your life stems from family, friends, a career or from your own standard, remember—you were wonderfully made. You have nothing to prove...because in Christ, our worth has already been proven. I dare you to take off your mask and start getting to know the woman God created when He lovingly formed you in His hands.

YOUR DAILY DARE

1. What secrets or hurts or fears are you hiding today?

2. What kind of masks are you wearing that keep you from healing?

3. What will it take for you to remove the mask and step into the authentic you?

dare to be MISUNDERSTOOD

by

DARE TO BE *MISUNDERSTOOD*

"Then the Lord opened the donkey's mouth and it said to Balaam, 'What have I done to you to make you beat me these three times?'"

Numbers 22:28 NIV

Balaam's donkey was a faithful, loyal, hardworking animal. By nature donkeys were known as beasts of burden. They carried the load. They weren't given to being unpredictable. However in this story, Balaam was taking a direction that God was displeased with. God interrupts Balaam's disobedience with an angelic visitation, which Balaam fails to see but his donkey can't avoid. Balaam's donkey finds herself with a choice: either to follow Balaam or to obey the angel of God. The story tells how the donkey dares to ignore Balaam's command and bow to the angel in her path, thus incurring an undeserved beating from a confused Balaam.

I have read and pondered on this many times not just because it's a great story... (Who doesn't love a talking donkey?) But more importantly this story teaches me that sometimes in order to do what's right you have to endure what's wrong. This donkey did not deserve the several beatings it received. It wasn't fair that the donkey was punished for obeying God, but so often in life, that's the way it is. When God asks us to obey, there's no guarantee that everyone around us will always agree or understand our actions. There are times in all of our journeys when we have to obey, thus daring to be misunderstood.

Sometimes we are so concerned to keep the Balaams of our life happy, we ignore the God whisper in our heart. We commit to keep carrying the load for Balaam, when God is asking us to drop the load for Him. We can never let Balaam's voice crowd out God's. True, it's hard at times to say no when there is a relationship, historically, where you always say yes, but if we ignore God we could also harm others with whom we do life. The donkey's disobedience that day would later prove to become Balaam's salvation.

In life we can't let the position of voices we listen to get confused. God's voice must be first. We can't let our desire to be understood silence the whispers of heaven. I remember when I was a teenager, I felt God pull me away from some friendships and ask me to spend more time with Him. I was misunderstood but I could not turn off this draw inside me to pursue Him even when I couldn't fully understand why. In hindsight I can see how this became a foundational time on my journey with God. I had to be misunderstood for a season, knowing that eventually the fruits of my decisions would be seen.

No one can be understood all the time. At times people didn't understand Jesus. Even His own parents misunderstood Him, like when He went to the temple as a boy. Our life can't always be explained in a satisfactory way to all concerned. We have to be bold enough to obey His call, even if that call contradicts what is popular or even deemed sensible. We have to dare to say yes to the things no one else sees, to speak of the whispers others have not heard and to act on the instructions no one else has received. Don't let our fear of being misunderstood stop us from acting. Everyone misunderstood Noah until the flood came. Mary was misunderstood and judged as a pregnant and unwed teenager. Jesus was misunderstood on the cross until the resurrection. Don't let your need for everything to be tidy remove God's promptings in your life.

Balaam's donkey was misunderstood, but eventually God let the donkey speak and when God opened her mouth she was shown faithful. I love how when the donkey spoke it was not resentful or hurtful to Balaam, even though he had been hurtful to her. When God let her speak, the donkey was faithful and gracious...revealing understanding to his misunderstanding.

We also have to commit to keep our hearts right. In a season when some would misunderstand us, we must trust in God. Let Him affirm you, so that when you speak He can be glorified and your actions justified.

God will always affirm those who dare to be misunderstood for His cause. So my friend, I dare you to heed that whisper you need to pay attention to. I dare you to respond to that heavenly nudge. I dare you to forget what people may say, remember God and do it anyway.

YOUR DAILY DARE

1. What path is God asking you to leave so you can follow Him?

2. Where do you need to be willing to be temporarily misunderstood?

3. What do you need to stop ignoring and start obeying?

dare to be LOVED

by ng

DARE TO BE *LOVED*

"The one who formed you says, 'I have called you by name. You are mine.'"

Isaiah 43:1 ESV

My twin daughters, Gracie & Bella, are awake for a maximum of 30 minutes in the mornings before they ask to put on one of their princess costumes. Their obsession with all things "princess" began about two years ago. We've seen all of the Disney classics, visited the Bippity-Boppity Boutique at Disneyland and spent a small fortune on princess dresses, shoes, tiaras, nightgowns, teacups...the list could go on and on! A few months ago, I overheard them in the playroom:

Gracie: "I'm the princess this time and it's *your* turn to play the prince."

Bella: "*You're* the prince. I can't be! Because I'M THE PRINCESS!"

Every girl wants to be the princess. But every girl also wants her prince. Born in to the heart of every human being is the deep desire to be loved. And as a mom to three little girls, and being one myself, I think a case could almost be made for the fact that girls have a double-dose, born-in need to be noticed, valued, pursued, cherished, known, *LOVED.* What's a princess without a prince? Whether school girls or grown women, we all dream of the "great romance."

This culture is constantly trying to define true love for us, because we're all looking for it. But instead of ever achieving this love that the world is trying to sell, we often feel beat down with reminders of standards we can't meet, beauty we can't attain and a love that we can't find. But love is not popularity. Love is not success. Love is not sex. Love is not a certain weight or brand. Real love is not a thing. It is a Person. We read in 1 John that, "This is real love; not that we loved God, but that He loved us and sent His Son as a sacrifice to take away our sins" (1 John 4:10 NLT). Through Christ's love, we realize that we are valued and cherished, created on purpose and with a purpose. Discovering this not only helps us find self-worth; it empowers us to walk stronger, fly higher and accomplish more than we ever thought possible. Even when life is disappointing, devastating, painful and confusing, God's love is the thread that holds us together.

All that our heavenly Father does is motivated by His everlasting love for us. His love is unending and eternal; a loving-kindness that will never dry up or run out. It is difficult for us to try and comprehend this kind of love and acceptance. No matter how many times you have felt rejected, unnoticed or unloved, know this: God is always relentlessly pursuing you. So let this truth permeate your mind and take root in your heart: The number one reason you were born is because God loves you.

Before you even took a breath, the Bible says that He knew you, loved you and designed your destiny (Psalm 139:13-16). As our Creator, God made us with a need for love. Then He showed us that our need can only be filled through a relationship with Jesus, knowing that Jesus gave His life so that we can experience real love. And when life is disappointing, devastating and painful, it is Christ's love that holds us together. His love takes our broken pieces and makes a work of art. We all desire to belong, to be accepted, to be known. Through Christ's love it is discovered that we are valued, cherished and favored.

The greatest romance this world has ever known is found in the way Christ demonstrated His love for us. He left the glories of heaven to live among us, sacrificed His life for us when He died on the cross and made a way for us to spend eternity with Him. There is no love more wildly passionate or extravagant than that.

Disney can't begin to create a love story so great. And better than the most romantic marriage proposal from your favorite movie, real love bends low and tenderly whispers, "I have called you by name. You are mine." Dare to accept this love. Dare to believe that you are adored, pursued and loved *completely*. When you do, it will change the way you act, the way you think and the way you live.

YOUR DAILY DARE

1. Are you holding onto an unrealistic concept of romance that's hindering your true search for love?

2. Do you accept the fact that God is head over heels in love with you? Unconditionally?

3. Pray that your heart can be opened to receiving love, cherishing love and returning it.

Day 18

dare to be A SERVANT

by CG

DARE TO BE *A SERVANT*

"The harvest is plentiful but the workers are few."
Matthew 9:37 NIV

In Matthew 9, Jesus is talking to His disciples about a problem He has observed—there is a vast harvest to be brought in but there are not enough workers. Jesus spent much of His time helping and serving people, bringing healing and life to hurting humanity. He went for days without rest or reprieve from the crowds that needed His help. However, on this particular day as He was amongst yet another crowd, He draws His disciples' attention to a worker-harvest ratio problem. To fully understand his point, let's go back a bit.

Mark 8 records how one day when Jesus was out teaching amongst the crowds of people with His disciples, He noticed the people were getting hungry and tired from the relentless heat of the day. Jesus turned to His disciples to ask what they could do to relieve the crowd's hunger: "Where can we get food for these people?" The disciples' reply came as something of a shock. Not only did they fail to suggest any solutions; they only added to the problem with their unwillingness to help. They let Jesus know that they were not in the catering business, nor was this their problem. Jesus was testing His disciples that day to see whether they had put limits on their willingness to serve. The disciples had somehow made following Jesus about selective service. Their work for Him may involve healing and teaching, but they drew the line at catering.

Add to the fact that in the crowd that day were over 5000 men, plus women and children. I am certain there were many people in that crowd who had the resourcefulness to help Jesus with this problem. However, it turned out that everyone had come that day to receive from Jesus, but no one was mindful that He might require something of them. No one volunteered to help feed the crowd. Everyone "observed" but no one "served." Because the task seemed so huge, people disqualified themselves from being part of the answer.

Turns out, Jesus was not looking for the qualified; He was looking for the willing. Enter a young boy who stepped forward and nervously offered his lunch to Jesus. He must have been only too aware that his lunch was not a viable solution to a problem of this size, yet his heart was saying, "I want to be a part of the answer. I want to serve!" I'm sure he had to overcome fears and embarrassment as he dared to approach Jesus. At the sight of this boy's servant heart, Jesus responded and used his morsel of food as the foundation of an incredible miracle.

Today, in so many ways, we can face the same problem. How many of those who describe themselves as a Jesus follower have actually become a Jesus server by helping others as He helped them? How many take the same good news that rescued them and use it to rescue someone else? We so often disqualify our contribution, thinking God is looking for the most skilled or professional when all He is looking for is someone to willingly play the part.

The design of heaven is that once we have been healed and restored, we in turn become carriers of that same healing to others. No one is too inexperienced, too old, young, busy or unnecessary. However, in our busy lives, all too often we can become Jesus watchers, rather than Jesus workers. We can attend church rather than be the church. We can often end up giving God a service slot instead of living our lives with a servant heart.

Jesus needs every follower to become a servant. So I dare you today in your heart to sign up again to be His worker. Serve Him in your church, your community and give your loaves and fishes without embarrassment. You will discover joy when He takes your contribution, however small, to start a miracle in the lives of others. Today, remove your excuses and be willing to step forward so that we can change the worker-harvest ratio and bring the harvest home.

YOUR DAILY DARE

1. Ask yourself, "Am I a worker or observer?"

2. What loaves and fishes can you contribute?

3. Where could you volunteer your time, skill and energy to reach more people?

dare to be CALLED OUT

by ng

DARE TO BE *CALLED OUT*

"For if you remain silent at this time, relief and deliverance for the Jews will arise from another place, but you and your father's family will perish. And who knows but that you have come to royal position for such a time as this?"

Esther 4:14 NIV

I often muse at the statistic claiming that the greatest fear among most Americans is public speaking. I suppose being, shall we say, not one to shy from a stage, I don't completely understand the fear. However, I do understand the fear of being called out. How many times did I sit in a classroom praying that the professor wouldn't call on me to expound on something for which I had no clue? And, how often have I told a half-truth or omitted information so as not to appear at fault or responsible? Sure, give me the limelight when you're applauding, but if you're admonishing or looking for a solution, please direct said light elsewhere.

I imagine Esther may have felt the same. The entire book of Esther is an anomaly, given that God is never referenced. That is a theological can of worms to be opened at another time. For now, there is enough within the framework of her story to teach us all a lesson in courage, bravery and faith.

The story opens with the King celebrating his wealth and power with a huge party (180-day party...he knew how to have a good time, apparently!). In the midst of the pomp and circumstance and who knows what else, the King requests that his wife Vashti come show off for his guests. She was beautiful, he was proud...and wanted others to know. For reasons unbeknownst to us, she refuses.

Oops. That made the king less than happy.

So, he did what many of us probably want to do from time to time—he got rid of the stubborn one and sought out a new one. I've always thought about his queen search as a sort of beauty pageant. One which EVERYONE had to enter. Esther, be it reluctantly or not, was crowned the new queen and began the 12 month beautification journey straight to the throne.

In the meantime, her Jewish family had somehow managed to offend the king's right hand man. Not the thing to do, especially given that man's response—let's kill all the Jews.

Now, Esther just so happened to be a Jew. The king just so happened not to know.

It soon became clear that the Jewish people were out of options and beseeched their queen to reason with her husband. One small caveat here...in those days, if anyone approached the king without an invitation, the king had the right to kill them—even those who were members of his family.

Everyone knew this. Esther definitely knew this. And, just like any of us would be, she was scared.

Enter Mordecai—the cousin who raised her...and the very Jew who had upset the royal cabinet member in the first place. Scared for himself, his family and his people, he very pointedly asks Esther a faith question—What if you were made queen so you could help save us? What if you're here for such a time as this?

Very often, we can find ourselves in similar situations...ones that make no sense...ones that scare us...In those moments, it's hard, if not impossible, to see God's logic or purpose. Those are the times that the spotlight doesn't lead to applause, but to vulnerability. Instead of being called out for an accomplishment or reward, maybe we are called out because we're playing a small part in a much bigger story.

Much like Esther, our circumstances often lead us to a point of critical decision...do we accept that which God has laid before us, despite the risk? Or do we shrink away to hide in the shadows?

I dare you to accept your mission. It may be uncomfortable, unpopular and even quite scary; but if we truly believe that God works all things together for His good, then we must claim the confidence that He didn't arbitrarily place us where we are. I dare you to not only listen for God's call on your life—but to respond.

Much like publicly speaking, you may incur sweaty palms, shortness of breath or some dizziness; but even in your most frightened state, never doubt that you are where you are on purpose.

Dare to act. Dare to respond. Dare to be called out.

YOUR DAILY DARE

1. What is God placing on your heart that requires action?

2. What is holding you back from fulfilling His desire?

3. Where can you respond boldly to His call on your life today?

dare to be PREPARED

by CG

DARE TO BE *PREPARED*

"Be prepared in season and out of season."

2 Timothy 4:2 NIV

"Be prepared in season and out of season." These famous words were spoken by the older, wiser apostle Paul to his younger student Timothy. Timothy was called to lead God's people, but before he could teach, train and build, he had to first show he was willing to prepare.

Preparation is an indication of what you are expecting. Show me a bride-to-be and I will show you her wedding magazines, her journal, fabric swatches and menu samples. Her expectation to marry has led her to prepare. Show me an expectant woman and you will find a prepared nursery, baby clothes and accessories. Why? Because preparation is the first indication of what you are daring to become.

This is why we must dare to prepare. We must commit to the process where we line up our lives with what our heart is expectantly awaiting, even if we can't see signs of what's to come. No woman resents preparing for her baby because she sees the visible signs that the baby is on its way. Yet spiritually, there is often no advance spiritual ultrasound that shows what's coming. This can make the preparation process less than exciting, and at times, even a little scary.

Just think about Noah, who was asked to prepare a boat for a flood that would be caused by relentless rain. He had never seen a boat or flood. He had no ultrasound picture to inspire him; he just had to obey. As others passed by laughing at the seemingly crazy old man, God smiled at Noah's willingness to dare to prepare. Or what about Sara who laughed at the very absurd thought of having a baby in her old age? She couldn't even imagine what that would look like, but she had to dare to conceive the idea before she could ever conceive the child.

Many years ago my husband and I were told by the doctors that we wouldn't be able to have children. The doctors said medically it wasn't something we should expect to happen. After my initial anger, frustration and shock at the devastating news, I remember crying even more tears when the realization hit me—I was not improving this diagnosis one bit by my reaction. My actions were only feeding my disappointment and confusion. I then realized I had the power to choose differently. So I chose to stop dwelling on the bad news and focus on God's good news for my future.

Steve and I decided that instead of giving up, we would dare to prepare our lives for a miracle. If we were going to believe God for a miracle, we better start preparing a life that could incubate one. We changed our prayers of anguish into prayers of faith. Isaiah 54:1 exhorts: "Sing oh barren woman." We took this advice and prepared our hearts by rejoicing with others who were pregnant. I started throwing baby showers for people that I barely knew. All that time, we were preparing the soil of our lives for our own miracle. It was five years later that God answered our prayers with the birth of our first child, our precious, prepared for, daughter, Hope Cherish.

What about you? What desire are you incubating that requires some preparation? When the apostle Paul was instructing his young disciple Timothy to get ready, he was saying, "Timothy, don't wait for the leadership badge. Lead now. Don't wait for the people to ask for your help. Prepare your life with wisdom and counsel now." Dare to prepare in private now for what God may use you to do in public later.

Advance preparation speaks of a life that believes. It is a commitment to something that hasn't even happened yet. It is faith in action. If I were to look at your life, what would your actions reveal to me about your forthcoming expectations? Instead of saying it might happen, prepare for it to happen. Today take some time to prepare your heart and soul. Write down areas where you need to begin the work of preparation. Let your spirit know that you aren't going to passively wait any longer for the thing your heart desires. Instead, you are going to dare to prepare.

YOUR DAILY DARE

1. Where does your faith await the action of preparation?
2. What areas can you identify where you need to stop delaying?
3. What preparation can you commit to today?

dare to

STAND YOUR GROUND

by ng

DARE TO *STAND YOUR GROUND*

"If we are thrown into the blazing furnace, the God we serve is able to deliver us from it, and He will deliver us from Your Majesty's hand. But even if He does not, we want you to know, Your Majesty, that we will not serve your gods or worship the image of gold you have set up."

Daniel 3:17,18 NIV

One of my favorite images in history is that of a small lady who refused to subjugate her morals to injustice. Her stance led to a humiliating arrest, but turned out to be a pivotal moment in the Civil Rights Movement in America. Of course, I'm referring to Rosa Parks. After digging up some facts about Ms. Parks and her actions that eventually led to a city-wide bus boycott, I was surprised to learn that she hadn't actually broken any law. It was the jaded, narrow attitude of the bus driver and city police that ultimately landed her behind bars. After 24 hours, she was bailed out by the president of the NAACP, Edgar Nixon, and instantly became a symbol of justice. The Montgomery bus boycott that ensued from her arrest lasted for 381 days, costing the city at least 75% of their typical revenue. Needless to say, she made her point.

When I think about Shadrach, Meshach and Abednego, I can't help but envision a very similar scenario. King Nebuchadnezzar had issued a decree demanding that at the sound of a horn, everyone had to kneel and worship him. (Quite the ego, no?) Shadrach, Meshach and Abednego knew the wrong in this decree. Out of loyalty to the one true God, they refused to bow down.

Now, I'd love to think that I would be just as resolute in such circumstances. But considering that everyone who violated the decree would be thrown into a blazing furnace, I would have to think long and hard about the pros and cons of the whole situation. I don't know if I would have the gumption and resolve to boldly violate this ridiculous law, knowing full well that a furnace awaited me. The three men in this story had the gumption. They believed that God would deliver them from their fate. And even if He didn't, they were resolute in their stance, refusing to deny their God by bowing to another.

What about us? Haven't we all been in scenarios that (we think) necessitate compromise? Haven't we all, from time to time, found it easier to stay quiet or just go with the flow for the risk of rocking the boat? I know personally there have been times when I've perceived the costs of standing my ground to outweigh the benefits. So, I stay quiet. I find ways and reasons to justify my actions, even when they're in direct contradiction to my convictions. In those moments, I try to think of the rest of this story. When the men were thrown into the furnace (which was heated so high the soldiers dropping them into it were killed!), they did not burn. In fact, they were joined by a fourth man and not only survived; they didn't have a hair singed or even a scent of smoke.

What does this mean? It means this very simple truth that so many of us, including myself, forget over and over—God honors our faith. Moreover, He not only sees our acts of faith; He sees the conviction in our hearts that point to Him. What a joy it must be for Him when we trust in His omnipotence, His righteousness and His salvation. And what a heartbreak when we don't.

Now, please hear me when I say that I highly doubt many of us out there are bent on contradicting God's sovereignty. But when it comes right down to it, a lot of us are OK with gray areas. After all, God can see that inside our hearts, we see things as black and white. What's the harm if we're a little gray on the outside? Besides, isn't it more loving, therefore most Christ-like not to offend someone by taking the moral high road?

Oh the games we play! We have only to see the end of the story of the men in the furnace to realize that—yes...our actions, though they seem innocent in light of the condition of our heart, matter. They are seen. Moreover, if we call ourselves Christians, all of our actions will be assumed to reflect Christ. When the men walked unharmed out of the furnace, the King who had made that decree in the first place saw the power of God and declared that anyone who spoke ill of Him would be put to death. That's an extreme example, obviously, but the message is clear—God is working all things for His good.

Much like Ms. Parks did so many years ago, when we stand strong, live boldly our convictions and remain faithful to what is right and just, despite the consequence, we are opening a window to the rest of the world to see God's faithfulness and deliverance. I dare you to be strong and bold and to hold your ground. I dare you to defy the risks, the scorn, the dangers of living your faith by staying true to God. And I dare you to believe that, despite our fears, God will use our faithfulness for His good.

YOUR DAILY DARE

1. Are you, or have you been in a situation that makes doing the right thing difficult?

2. Do you compromise your faith for the sake of fitting in, or at least, not standing out?

3. Where in your life do you need to hold firm? Pray for the strength and wisdom to do so.

dare to be LIMITLESS

by cg

DARE TO BE *LIMITLESS*

"Go around and ask all your neighbors for empty jars. Don't ask for just a few."

2 Kings 4:3 NIV

The story of the widow in 2 Kings 4 is one of my favorite pictures of how God is not just enough; but He will always be *more* than enough. In this story, a woman who has been widowed finds herself faced with crippling debt and in fear for her future. Creditors are coming to take her sons away in lieu of payment. The story doesn't make clear how long this situation had been going on, but clearly the circumstances had worsened over time. Her life had become suffocated by fear and now in desperation the widow cries out to the prophet Elisha to help her in her plight. This cry for help marks the first time the widow dares to break the silence and shame that the limitation of her debt had contained within her for so long. She allowed her natural limitations to contain her spirit and became crippled and intimidated by debt. Just like her, we can also become limited by circumstances that interrupt our lives; situations that seem to shut us down and cut short our destiny.

This widow's story provides us with great insight as to how our God deals with our frequently limited perspective of life. We, like this widow, have to be willing to dare to break limitations by being obedient to God. We have to take some of the same steps this widow took in 2 Kings 4. First, she had to push past the restrictions of her own pride and embarrassment. When she cried out for help she was breaking the silence and removing its limiting power. Often, it is our refusal to cry out that keeps us locked up. We need to be willing to seek help from those who have the ability to move us forward. This woman cried out to a prophet of God—a man who had seen many limitation-removing miracles take place. When faced with a mountain challenge, we need to ask for help from those who have mountain climbing experience.

After the widow had cried out, there came the challenge of re-evaluating her limitations as Elisha asked her in verse 2, "What do you have in your house?" The widow was confused at the question. She had become so aware of what she didn't have, that she had overlooked what she did have. Her reply to Elisha is, "Your servant has nothing except a little oil." The truth is limitation makes us question every area of our lives. We often devalue any contribution when we feel overwhelmed by life. Yet we have to dare to look again. Don't believe the lies of the limitation. If you are lacking in one area look for what you have in another. She may not have had money, but she had a little oil, which until Elisha had asked her, she had overlooked.

Elisha then instructed her to find more empty jars, to add to her emptiness. This seems a strange instruction, to add more lack when the widow was already overwhelmed with need. Perhaps we would be more open to go ask our neighbors for money or provisions, to at least lessen our problem; but God's answer was to increase the need. Elisha was about to demonstrate to this widow that the only limitation is our ability to trust Him. His supply only ended with the widow's inability to find more emptiness to fill.

We have to dare to remove our limitations—to not allow life and all its complexities remove our ability to keep pushing our faith to new places. We have to determine we will stretch further and believe for greater. When limitation is telling us to quiet down, we, like this widow, have to dare to call out, dare to present God with our little, knowing He is our more than enough. We must commit even in times of need to still be willing to find more needs for God to fill. If the widow hadn't cried out, it would have been a death sentence for her family. So what about you? Where do you introduce limitation to your limitless God?

YOUR DAILY DARE

1. Where do you need to dare to cry out today and address your limitations?

2. Where do you need to look again for what you have to start your miracle?

3. What emptiness can you believe God to fill?

dare to be FEARLESS

by ng

DARE TO BE *FEARLESS*

"Don't be afraid...those who are with us are more than those who are with them."
2 Kings 6:16 NIV

Most of us don't like to admit when we're afraid. Be it fear of relationships, circumstances, failure or even victory, most times we suppress our fear from the outside in. Or at least we try to. No one likes to admit weakness, be it justified or not. This world doesn't honor or reward weakness and fear. It exalts those who appear to be brave, self-assured...those who don't need anyone or anything to get by.

What a tragedy! Because of our best efforts to hide our fear, we suppress it, camouflage it and even rename it to the point that we don't even recognize it anymore. At that point, we can't root it out or find a solution. It's only when we name our fears and own them that we can begin to move past them. And even then, we must still come to the realization that we can't do it without God. Fortunately, we don't have to. In God's perfect wisdom, creation and plan, He crafted us to depend on Him for everything—from the very breath we breathe to the most difficult, scariest circumstance we will face. It's within that dependence that we can truly begin to lay our fears down.

In 2 Kings, we read about Elisha and his servant. In the night, an army of chariots and horses has surrounded the city in which they're staying. Naturally, the servant is terrified. That's when Elisha drops those three little words that are much easier to shrug off as the musings of a crazy man than to grasp and own. "Don't be afraid."

Now, I don't know about you; but if I woke up tomorrow morning with my home surrounded by chariots, I think I'd freak out a bit. But here's the kicker. Elisha wasn't just paying lip service to an idea of fearlessness. He saw the greater workings of God. He was confident in God's protection and provision. And he prayed that his servant would also see what he saw—an army of angels and chariots of fire. The army of the Lord was infinitely greater than that of the enemy.

The same is true today. We may not be surrounded by literal enemy chariots and armies, but we are immersed in a culture that celebrates self-reliance and admonishes failure. At times, the pressure to be good, successful, beautiful, etc., can send us into a spiritual and emotional paralysis. We learn that we're supposed to figure out this thing called life on our own...but we're also so terrified of the possibility of failure, that we more often than not do nothing. Fear becomes our constant companion and a cumbersome anchor. As we settle into our self-appointed role of wall-flower, watching life pass us by, we easily forget the promises in scripture. The promises that say we're not given a spirit of fear and timidity, but one of power, love and self-control. (2 Tim 1:7)

Did you catch that? Power. Love. Self-control.

These are the tools that will root out fear in your life. These are the tools that manifest in your heart when you surrender your life to the one who casts out fear—the one who has sent angel armies of fire to guard our lives and our hearts.

Fearlessness has little to do with us. It has everything to do with Him. And through Him, we can walk tall and proud and through life's storms and trials, because we're not doing it alone. I dare you to examine the fears in your life and heart. Where do they originate? How are they controlling you? How are they robbing you of a life lived in the confidence of the Holy Spirit? You were not meant to live a life of fear. God wants more for you and created you for it. We all face fear in our lives...yesterday, today and tomorrow...and that's OK. Just don't dwell in it. Own it...then surrender it and rest in the power of your God—who has already defeated and conquered every fear in this world.

YOUR DAILY DARE

1. What fears are clouding your heart and mind today?

2. When is the last time you allowed yourself to admit your own fears to God? To yourself?

3. What are ways that you can begin to surrender the fear in your life?

dare to

OWN YOUR ZONE

by cg

DARE TO *OWN YOUR ZONE*

"A little sleep a little slumber a little folding of the hands to rest and poverty will come on you like a thief and scarcity like an armed man."

Proverbs 24:33 NIV

This Proverb describes a man who has been given the opportunity of taking a vineyard full of potential and turning it into a profitable field of crops. Yet we don't read of this field making any profit or producing anything of use for its owner; rather, we read that it has become a place that is overgrown, rampant with weeds, thorns and thistles.

I wonder how often the same picture could be drawn of our lives. God has also entrusted to each of us a life filled with dormant potential...a life that, just like that vineyard, we are given to tend and to grow. Yet often because of the circumstances of life, our own insecurities, fears and at times neglect, much like the man in this Proverb, we can fail to ever see that full potential realized.

As women we have to dare to "own our zone." We need to recognize that where God has planted us is our "zone." We have a life that is ours to shape. You may have a marriage to nurture or children that are yours to love and invest in. Your zone may include a business, ministry or relationships for which you have responsibility. We often have to stop looking around at what everyone else is doing, and instead take the time to focus afresh on "our zone" and ask, "Am I owning it?"

A while ago, we were planning a short break with our children. It was the night before we were due to leave when all of a sudden our son, Noah Brave, became very ill. With a spiking temperature and sore tummy I sent him to bed, hoping the sleep would settle him down. Later that night, I went into his room and kissed his very hot head and prayed quietly for him to recover. As I left his bedroom I felt the spirit of God say to me, "Is that it?" "Is that what, Lord?" I replied. I felt God challenge me to the core, "Is that all the prayer you are going to pray over your son in your house?"

It was in that moment I felt God was trying to awaken me to my own apathy and I began to realize that God has entrusted me to look after, protect and own my zone. I awakened again to the truth that the enemy has no right to attack my children, and this sickness does not belong in my household! I needed to remove the apathy that had crept into my heart and take the authority that I had been given in Christ. I re-entered Noah's room as he lay fast asleep, only this time I was not going to pray politely—now this momma was going to pray passionately. I stood in his room and dared to own the zone. I prayed with authority and claimed healing for his sick body. I spoke words of strength over him as he slept and commanded him to be well. As I closed my prayer I said, "In the name of Jesus," and to my surprise, Noah from his deep sleep shouted, "Amen!"

I will never forget the power of God that night; the presence of God was so tangible. Even though Noah's body was asleep, clearly his spirit was wide awake and declaring "Amen" to his mom finally owning her zone. I learned a lesson that night that, as a mother, I could either let in apathy or take authority.

Jesus one time went into His father's house, to worship. We read in Matthew 21:12 that as He entered He found there were money lenders and vendors who had set up their stalls where people should have been worshipping. At the sight of this, Jesus became angry. This was not the kind of behavior that belonged in His father's house. It records that "zeal for the house consumed him," as Jesus turned tables and threw out the money exchangers. He wasn't having a bad day or throwing a temper tantrum; He was "owning his zone." He was showing compromise the door and restoring righteousness and order. And we must commit to do the same.

So where has apathy let the enemy move into your zone? What are you putting up with that you need to stand up to? Where are weeds growing instead of vines? Decide today you are going to dare to protect, defend, stand strong, pray, nurture and produce a great harvest in your zone. Dare today to "own your zone."

YOUR DAILY DARE

1. Where do you need to remove apathy?

2. What is in your zone that you need to identify and own?

3. Where do you need to pray differently and awake the dormant potential?

dare to

NOT SETTLE

by ng

DARE TO *NOT SETTLE*

"The thief comes only to steal and kill and destroy; I have come that they may have life, and have it to the full."

John 10:10 NIV

Do you remember when you were younger and your dreams and plans for the rest of your life seemed to reach straight to the moon? You were going to be an actress or an astronaut and probably score an Olympic gold medal on your way to the White House, right? Yet somewhere between Barbies and prom night and mommyhood, your vision seems to have been reigned in a bit. Gone are the dreams of seeing our name in lights or finding the cure for cancer or some other monumental, world-changing achievement. They've been replaced by car pools, mortgage payments, diapers to change and deadlines to meet. Your dreams of an epic romance have likely also been sidelined for a date night once a month—maybe—and the hope that maybe this year you won't have to plan your own romantic anniversary date.

Seems to me like our expectations have lowered a bit (a lot). And while some of that is just a natural progression as we grow up and get to know what our world is really like, some of that seems, just a bit, like giving up. Somehow, I don't think that's what God had in mind when He placed us here on earth. When I read that He came to give us life to the full, I believe that He really does want us to have a life full of our hopes and dreams and happiness. I don't think He wants those who claim to be His walking around with our heads drooped, shoulders stooped, stressed to the max because of all that life is heaping upon us. And I say that knowing full well that I am one of the greatest perpetrators! Very often, I resign myself to being stressed, frenzied and, generally, just doing what I have to do everyday to get by. After all, I'm a working mom. I have endless deadlines and endless demands of my time. Surely God sees that my shoulder is to the grindstone and I'm going full-tilt to make sure ends are met. Surely that's enough...right? Well, to be honest...I think the answer is no. It's not that we're not trying hard enough; it's that we're trying so hard for the wrong things.

Now, I'm sure many of you are shaking your heads thinking—wait. Your name is in lights. You have achieved your dreams. You have a wonderful husband and family. And you are absolutely right about all of that. But despite all of those facts, I still allow myself to get mired down by stuff and, instead of enjoying the blessings God has heaped upon me, I get stressed out, worn out and drained. Soon, there's little left within me that feels joyous or, at times, even thankful. For sure, that is not what God intended for me or for you. And, when we are walking hand in hand with Him, depending on His strength and wisdom for each day, we don't tend to experience the sheer exhaustion of life at every turn. It's when we take on the weight of our world and everyone else's all by ourselves that things start to fall apart.

As women, perhaps we, more than men, feel the need to prove that we can do it...and we can do it all without any help from anyone. So stand back, for I am woman...hear me roar. Right? (Please tell me I'm not the only one!) For some reason, we have within us this drive to prove that we can be Super Mom and Super Wife and Super Everything with little more than a caffeine buzz to get us through. We are tragically wrong. Not only can we not handle everything we try to juggle on our own; we often get indignant and defensive about our performance or how we're the only ones who remember how to load the dishwasher or remember to call and schedule the kids' doctor appointments, etc., etc., until it's us against the world.

Call it the martyrdom mommy lament. We feel alone, because we don't ask for help. We feel stressed because we've taken on way too much—just to prove that we can. And we feel unhappy and un-romanced and unloved because we've let our imaginations and pop culture set a bar that's not only unrealistic; it's not in line with God's purpose for our lives or hearts.

It's time to put on the brakes. It's time to sit down with your kids, your husband and your God and decide as a family what's working and what's not. What's feeding your souls and what's draining them? God wants us to have mountaintop experiences. He wants us to be giddy with romance and excitement. On His terms. God didn't create you to be a task-master or a work horse. He created you to experience all of His creation and to enjoy Him because He loves you!

So today, I dare you not to settle for getting by. I dare you not to make your to-do list be your gauge of satisfaction in your life. And I dare you not to go it alone. You are fearfully and wonderfully made—just like everyone else. Invite some other wonderful creations into your heart and your life. Ask for help. Be grateful for the blessings and always expect more than you can even imagine.

YOUR DAILY DARE

1. Are there areas in your life where you've grown complacent?

2. Are there certain goals, emotions or dreams that you've tabled, assuming that your window to experience or achieve them is long gone?

3. Today, take note of three things in your life you're thankful for and look for one thing in your life to aim for—be it a part-time job, a musical endeavor, going back to school, etc. Dare to let God help you not to settle and pray that He show you the path towards your goals.

dare to be INVOLVED

by cg

DARE TO BE *INVOLVED*

"Finally Paul became so annoyed that he turned around and said to the spirit, 'In the name of Jesus Christ I command you to come out of her!'"

Acts 16:18 NIV

Involvement is not something we typically take on lightly. The word "involvement" automatically makes us think of demands, giving of our time and resources. It suggests a commitment beyond where we may feel comfortable. I have found in life that what I am involved with shapes much of my time, space and decisions. That is why every now and again, I have to dare myself to press refresh on what I am choosing to be involved with.

Jesus came not just to invite people to follow him, nor did He come to interfere in people's lives. He came to get involved. He came to bring clarity into confusion and draw purpose out of pain.

When Jesus said, "follow me" to His disciples, this was just their first step into what would become a lifelong involvement. Up until then, these young men had for the most part spent more hours with fish than with people. Now, they were not only daring to respond to Jesus' invitation; they were daring to be involved in His mission. Jesus took them from the calm, tranquil lake into a frantic sea of hurting humanity, where their involvement now looked like healing the sick, feeding the hungry and helping the hurting.

We read in Matt 4 that on their first day on the job, Jesus immersed them into their new calling. He wasn't asking them to preach sermons at people, but to get amongst the people and serve them. God designed your life and mine for this same "great involvement." We were created to be an answer to the problem, a light in the darkness. Therefore, if we are to truly discover what it means to follow Him, we must dare to keep stepping outside of ourselves into the lives of those around us.

How many times do we resist involvement because we are afraid of the workload it may lead us into? The encouraging news is we are not alone in this! Some of the greatest heroes of the faith also had to push past their excuses and reluctances and dare to be involved. In Acts 16, we read a story that illustrates this well. The apostle Paul finds himself being followed by a demon-possessed slave girl. She follows him with shouts and jeers as he is ministering to the people of the town. The shocking part of this story is it takes three days of this persistent annoyance before Paul decides he will get involved and deliver the girl from her torment.

It seems hard to comprehend that the great apostle Paul would ignore this poor girl's plight for so long. Perhaps an explanation as to why Paul delayed was because he knew first-hand that once he got involved in this girl's life, the trouble that was following her would soon be following him. Sure enough, when Paul finally steps in, he begins a chain reaction of events that eventually lead to him being thrown into prison. Herein lies our reason for so often avoiding involvement. We may not end up in prison as Paul did, but when we get involved with our neighbors who are in crisis or the mom at the school facing cancer, or the family crippled by debt, it is the beginning of accepting a responsibility to become part of the answer. It is so much easier to pray from a distance. But involvement closes the gap between the prayer and the person and asks us to participate in the healing process.

As women, we must push past the fear of inconvenience and dare to be involved because involvement is often the very doorway through which miracles happen. It was, if you remember, Paul's involvement with this slave girl that moved God to intervene in the prison cell that Paul later found himself in and bring about Paul and Silas' miraculous jailbreak which led to all of the jailer's family coming to Christ!

We so often want to experience the jailbreak miracles without the slave girl deliverance, but these two incidents are linked. God saves some of His best answers for those who will dare to get involved in another's questions.

So friend, what are you waiting for? I dare you to get involved today. Who knows what miracles, new relationships or God-opportunities are on the other side of your involvement? I am so grateful that one day someone got involved in my life and led me to meet Jesus. He didn't just enter my heart, but involved Himself in every area of my life; transforming my world forever. Girls, its our turn to go and do the same.

YOUR DAILY DARE

1. Where is your involvement stuck? What new places could you dare to be involved in?

2. What need are you ignoring that is crying out for your help?

3. What load do you need to be willing to help another carry today?

dare to be HIS

by ng

DARE TO BE *HIS*

"Peter replied, 'Man, I don't know what you're talking about!' Just as he was speaking, the rooster crowed. The Lord turned and looked straight at Peter."

Luke 22:58-61 NIV

Have you ever had to take sides in an argument between two friends or family members? Awkward, isn't it? When you're with the one, you want to sympathize with them and rally behind them. And when you're with the other, you might feel like doing the same. Trouble is, by riding the fence, you can't really commit to either friend and end up relying on some kind of deception to keep each one happy.

Life and God work like that a lot, so it seems. In our politically correct culture it's become increasingly unpopular to be a Christian. You can be spiritual; you just can't name one God as the only God, meaning all the other gods are false. That's just not cool. Sadly, that's just not true. We know there is the one true God. We know the great lengths to which He went in order to have a relationship with each of us. Moreover, we know His unconditional, relentless love. Still, when it comes time for us to pick a side and stand firmly for that which we know is truth, more often than not, we shy away. At times, we flat out deny our association with Christ altogether. Sound familiar?

Whenever I read the story of Peter's denial, I cringe. Especially when it states that after the third denial, the Lord looked directly at him. Just wrap your head around that for a minute. Earlier that very day, Jesus tells Peter he will deny Him three times...which, of course, Peter profusely denies. And then, when the rest of the world decided that they'd had it with Jesus—that very day—Peter does just that. He denies His Lord three times...and then, seemingly out of nowhere, Jesus' eyes find his.

Again, I get chills when I think about the eyes of Jesus looking directly into my own after denying Him. And then, I realize that I'm not so deeply affected just because this happened to Peter; I know I have been Peter. Through my action, inaction, words or silence, at various points in my life, I have denied my savior. And every time, I have felt the eyes of Jesus looking into mine. They aren't judgemental or condemning; they do not have to be. The loving eyes of Jesus peering into the lying eyes and heart of mine are enough to make my breath catch as I look upon the distance I am creating between Jesus and myself.

What's more...Jesus prepared us for the world's rejection. He knew we would be ostracized, ridiculed and worse because of our love for Him. He knew our journey with Him in this world would be difficult and, at times, painful—much like His own. He knew and He told us so. Still, when adversity arises, we almost always seem shocked and victimized. And who wants to feel like a victim? Especially when it's so much easier to just look the other direction, hope no one realizes you're with Christ and just get through life without too much discomfort...

But that's not what God desires from us. And that's not what He deserves. While we may feel centuries removed and disconnected from Peter and his denial with the Son of God on His way to the cross, we are faced every single day with the radical truth of the cross and resurrection. Much like Peter, truth is right in front of us; yet we still hesitate to give or reveal our allegiance to Christ. I'm not saying that our day to day involves an encounter of such grave circumstance as Peter's. But go with me here... Picture this:

The last time a group of co-workers sat around gossiping about someone else—and you stayed silent...

When some of your friends share tales of a wild Saturday night...and you don't share your much more "boring" preparation for church the next day...

Or the last time you saw someone in need and simply turned the other way...

Opportunity is before us all the time to demonstrate the light and love of the one who lives within us. But when we avoid it for fear of embarrassment, inconvenience or any other such mundane excuse, we're acting much like Peter. And God is watching our every move.

So today, I dare you to stop avoiding opportunities to proclaim that you belong to God. Rather, jump on them! I dare you to let the world know that you are His—redeemed, changed, loved—and you are not ashamed or put out to be so; rather, I dare you to truly be a proud child of the King.

YOUR DAILY DARE

1. Why do you hesitate to let others know you are a Christian?

2. What environments are you in regularly that you have been concealing or, at least, staying quiet about your faith?

3. What are the attributes of God that you are most proud of and in love with? Write them down. Carry them with you and never, ever be ashamed to be His.

Day 28

dare to be

KIND

by

DARE TO BE *KIND*

"A kindhearted woman gains honor."

Proverbs 11:16 NIV

Flicking through the pages of my life, the people and places that most often stand out are those marked by kindness. It's the times when someone has interrupted my usual with an unusual act of generosity, favor and thoughtfulness, that mark moments. I remember one such time was the evening when my husband romantically proposed to me in a small French village. At the table next to ours was a beautiful French family who, though they didn't speak any English, understood our moment of celebration and without wanting any recognition, quietly took care of paying for our bill as they discreetly left the restaurant. They were complete strangers, yet through an act of generosity many years ago, they became part of our story that I am still telling today.

Kindness has the power to write your life into the pages of others. It is a doorway that can open the most broken hearts; it is a key that can unlock the most guarded doors. Proverbs 11:16 tells us that it's the kindness of our heart that will gain the respect of others. People can be dismissive or even disrespectful of another's values, beliefs or cause, but I have yet to find anyone who won't make way when kindness enters the room.

I remember one time when we were struggling with a neighbor in our community. They always seemed to complain about anything and everything—from people parking in their way, to children picking the wrong tree to climb or the dog barking just one time too many. It was apparent that this neighbor was unhappy to share the same street with anyone since all the other neighbors had experienced some complaint at some time.

After many conversations with my husband about their perpetual bad attitude, I decided that I would try a different approach. Instead of getting frustrated, I was going to dare to be the one who was kind. I started praying for this person. That led to me having kinder thoughts about them, then the tension lessened and my compassion increased. I found myself picking up extra groceries for them at the store or flowers for their home.

Slowly, week by week, I deliberately planned an act of kindness towards my neighbor. My whole family got involved; the kids would help move their garbage bins, the dog would wag its tail instead of barking. I visibly saw kindness begin to melt the deep freeze that life had put on them. It wasn't long until this neighbor was on good terms with everyone on the street, and the same kindness that had been sown into their life they now started expressing towards others.

Christ has called us to be carriers of kindness; to close the gap that selfishness can cause in our society, to demonstrate a love that can be seen in kind actions and heard in kind words. For many people kindness is something they rarely see and even less frequently have had expressed towards them. Too many lives are void of the kiss of kindness. A kind life is not one that makes a one-off gesture; it's a life that smiles each day at the possibility that kindness could open.

Proverbs 31 describes a beautiful and virtuous woman. She is a wife and a mother who her family calls "blessed." It says in verse 20 that she "extends her hands to the poor and needy." This woman exemplifies kindness in all areas of life. If we want people in our world to call us blessed, I believe we have to have a hand and life that extends to others daily.

Kindness is a decision that comes from a heart that puts others first. Kindness will leave a trail in the lives of those around you that leads them to God. Romans 2:4 says that "Kindness leads to repentance!' Jesus' kindness led people to salvation and caused people to become his followers. When we model the same behavior we can have the same results. Kindness can be time-consuming and demand you to give and to love even when you don't feel like it. But, kindness builds a legacy in your life. it changes individuals and communities. So I dare you today to leave a trail of kindness that reflects the kindness of our God who extends goodness to us every day.

YOUR DAILY DARE

1. Are your thoughts, speech, motives and actions, led by kindness?
2. Where can you use the key of kindness to unlock a situation?
3. What act of kindness can you extend today to a person in your life?

dare to be CONFIDENT

by ng

DARE TO BE *CONFIDENT*

"God said, 'I will be with you.'"
Exodus 3:12 NIV

Oscar Wilde once said, "Be yourself; everyone else is already taken." I've always loved that quote. But through the years, the thought of just being myself has, at times, been utterly terrifying. Sure, it sounds like such a wonderful notion to be true, genuine, authentic. But instead it has often seemed easier to pretend to be a much better version of the real me.

Years ago, when I felt the urging in my spirit to pursue full-time music ministry, words were spoken over me that strangled my courage. I allowed these words to take up residence in my heart and mind, and insecurity began to take over. I had always felt such a strong calling on my life to use music as a way to share the hope and peace of Jesus Christ. The time had finally come for me to step out in faith, and begin to pursue my God-given dream. As I shared these hopes and dreams with the person who was a leader and musical mentor in my life at the time, I will never forget his first response: "That will never work. You're not good enough. There is nothing particularly special about you."

Of course I never let it show how badly those words hurt me. But they haunted me. Slowly but surely I began to believe them, and instead of embracing who God made and called me to be, I decided I would try to be anything other than myself.

Being vulnerable seemed far too risky, so I tried to become what I thought would be more "acceptable." Driven by my hope to look better, sing greater, sound more spiritual, my fear of rejection and desperate need to be accepted stifled my courage to be myself. These things became like different disguises or masks, painting what I thought was a better version of who I really was.

Because the real me was broken. Scarred. A girl who struggled with an eating disorder for years. Those words that had been spoken over me led me down a path of doubt, self-hatred, shame and fear. The loud voice in my head would scream: "You are not good enough." I allowed that thought to choke out the truth—that I was created for a reason. I had forgotten that God thinks beautiful and wonderful thoughts about me, and that He had created me to be wonderfully complex.

Insecurity is the uneasy, unsettled and fearful awareness of the gap between who I want to be and who I am. Insecurity isn't just defeating—it's dangerous. It can keep us from embracing who God has created each one of us to be, and hinder us from engaging in our God-designed destiny.

God gives us a beautiful example of someone who struggled with insecurities and doubt in the person of Moses, who has long been one of my favorite characters of the Bible. Read Exodus chapters 3 & 4. God performed miraculous signs and wonders for Moses. But when God instructed him on what to do for his people, Moses doubted. Fear stepped in and he wondered what people would think. He felt inadequate and afraid.

It was time for Moses to step out in faith. God had chosen to use Moses to lead His people—the more than two million descendants of Jacob who were living as slaves in Egypt—back to the Promised Land. God said: "Now go, I am sending you to Pharaoh to bring My people, the Israelites, out of Egypt." (Exodus 3:10 NIV)

Moses' response in Exodus 4:1: "But they will not believe me or listen to my voice..." (ESV)

This is one of the first times we see Moses' insecurity on display. I so "get" Moses, because I often feel this gap between who I am and who I think I need to be. In later verses, we see his continued uncertainty and doubt: "Master, Please. I don't talk well. I've never been good with words." (Exodus 4:10 MSG)

But God replied with these comforting words: "I will help you speak and teach you what to say." (Exodus 4:12 NIV)

Insecurity is the uneasy, unsettled, and fearful awareness of the gap between who I want to be and who I am. Most of us will feel something like this at some point today, if you haven't already: "I'm not enough; I don't have it." That anxious, uneasy, unsettled, fearful feeling threatens to take over. But remember this: It is His unrelenting grace that gives the courage to shake that off. In those moments of self-pity and fear, God is speaking. But are we listening? He who spoke us in to existence, is speaking now.

The following is from Brenan Manning's profound book, *Posers, Fakers, and Wannabes* and perfectly articulates what I believe God says to all of us: "Come out of self-hatred into my love. Come to me now. Forget about yourself. Accept who I am for you—your rescuer—endlessly loving, forever patient, unbearably forgiving...I will not crush you. I will not extinguish you. For once and forever, relax: you are safe with me."

You are *His* daughter. Hear your Father whisper this in your ear, "I created you and I did a fabulous job. You are valued, loved and cherished. I will equip you, and most of all—I will be with you."

Repeat this after me: "I am who God says that I am." Now, I dare you to go walk in that strength. Stand taller and let a God-infused confidence guide you today.

YOUR DAILY DARE

1. What negative words have been spoken over your life? Now take your pen and draw a line through those words. Then write these: "I AM WHO GOD SAYS THAT I AM."

2. What insecurities am I allowing to overtake my heart?

3. Do I trust God when He says that I am wonderfully made? Do I believe that He did NOT make a mistake when He made me?

dare to be A FINISHER

by cg

DARE TO BE *A FINISHER*

"Now finish the work so that your eager willingness to do it may be matched by your completion of it."
2 Corinthians 8:11 NIV

Everyone loves a strong start. There's a certain rush of adrenaline and excitement that accompanies a new task, idea or commitment. Do you remember the last time you set out to organize every bit of clutter in the house? Or the last time you joined a gym, started a cleanse and launched a new diet? The first few days are great! The novelty of the idea or task presses us on. Over time, however, that novelty wears off and soon, what was once new is now mundane and no longer very interesting.

We are often enthusiastic starters, but there is a special joy that God wants us to experience—the joy of completion. The joy of seeing that the work was worth it... The joy of surveying your work from a distance and seeing a job well done... But such joy isn't easy to come by. Much like a marathon, we have to endure pain and struggle and fatigue and press on even when we feel like quitting. We must dare to be women who not only start well; but finish well. We must dare to cross the finish line.

I love the story of the Good Samaritan who helped the injured man on the side of the road. When no one else would stop, he did. He bandaged his wounds...but he didn't stop there. He took him to an inn where he was fed and cared for. And the next day, he came back to pay for any other costs involved in this man's full restoration. The Good Samaritan finished well.

The Word tells us that, "He who began a good work in you will see it through to completion." For us to be true followers of Jesus, then we have to learn how to follow His commitment to finish well. Jesus stuck with His disciples on both their best and worst days. He never threatened to leave them even when they chose to leave Him. From doubting Thomas, to a denial from Peter and a betrayal from Judas, Jesus was surrounded by people who didn't finish what they started. And yet, He didn't let their failure deter the completion of the work He had begun in each of them. His commitment was and is unconditional. He is the ultimate finisher. Remember in those last agonizing moments as Jesus hung on the cross, He didn't hang His head or breathe His last breath until He uttered the words "It is finished." He left no captive bound; no sin unforgiven; no enemy undefeated. He endured death until victory was won and our eternity secure.

So what about you and me? I'm often aware of many things left undone in my life. Relationships with no closure...Hurts untreated...Loose ends abound! However, we are called to be finishers. We should be the modern-day Samaritans, modeling the character of a Savior who always ends well. In our communities and families, we should be known as those who care enough to stay with people through the good and the bad. Our words should be reliable. Our commitments, as strong at the end as they are at the beginning... We should embody the words from the Apostle Paul and run our race until we gain our crown at the finish line.

I dare you today to take an inventory of the things that you need to complete. Where are the loose ends in your life? What promises have you made that remain to be met? Projects, promises and relationships all need to have the joy of completion. Don't let your life read like an unfinished sentence. See it through to the end and dare to discover the joy of being a finisher.

YOUR DAILY DARE

1. What areas do you need to commit to complete?

2. Where have you left doors open that need to be closed?

3. Who is on your path that needs you to be their Good Samaritan?

FOR MORE RESOURCES

by Natalie Grant & Charlotte Gambill please visit:

www.daretoberevolution.com/store
Twitter.com/daretobeevent
Facebook.com/daretobetour

For Dare To Be apparel please visit:
www.daretoberevolution.com/store

OTHER RESOURCES BY NATALIE GRANT:

THE REAL ME *book*
LOVE REVOLUTION *cd*
RELENTLESS *cd*

OTHER BOOKS BY CHARLOTTE GAMBILL:

NOW WHAT?
IN HER SHOES
IDENTITY

ABOUT THE AUTHORS

NATALIE GRANT

Grammy nominated Christian vocalist and multi Dove Award winner, Natalie Grant, is a singer-songwriter from Nashville, TN. Natalie's work has gained international acclaim, including five Dove Awards for Female Vocalist of the year. Natalie is married to producer Bernie Herms and they have three children Grace Ana, Isabella Noelle and Sadie Rose.

twitter.com/nataliegrant
www.nataliegrant.com

CHARLOTTE GAMBILL

Charlotte Gambill is an international speaker and author, best known for her practical and passionate application of God's word. Her messages of life and purpose are rallying a generation to embrace the broken and become ambassadors of hope. Charlotte and her husband Steve, are the lead Pastors at Life Church, England—www.lifechurchhome.com. They have two children, Hope Cherish and Noah Brave.

twitter.com/charlgambill
www.charlottegambill.com